I don't know how many times I h~~~~ ~~~~ ~~ ~~~~, ~~~ ~~~~~ *talk about that in seminary.* While it is impossible to talk about everything, especially in an ever-changing society, Drs. Dean and Hughes have broached many of the subjects that perplex even the tenured pastor. In *Together We Lead*, their approach is thoroughly biblical. Whether analyzing the call to ministry, models of leadership, or dealing with major church conflict, Drs. Dean and Hughes first point to the Scriptures instead of their own experience or the latest trends. In addition to being thoroughly biblical, their treatment is purposefully practical. Starting with the question of *What does the church need today?* and sprinkling thought-provoking questions and case studies along the way, every reader will find a practical book for ministry leadership in a complex and changing world.

—Dr. Steve Horn,
Executive Director, Louisiana Baptists

Dean and Hughes perfectly complement one another. Their book is infused with biblical examples, case studies, practical helps, and timeless leadership principles. *Together We Lead* is an exceptional leadership resource that can be used for personal growth, team development, and mentoring opportunities!

—Dr. Scott Sullivan,
Discipleship Catalyst, Georgia Baptist Mission Board

Everything rises or falls on leadership! Adam Hughes and Jody Dean have given us a leadership book that understands the roles both leadership and management play in the local church. Here are biblical principles expressed in practical ways that will help any pastor to both lead and administrate and do it well. Highly recommended.

—David L. Allen, Distinguished Professor of Preaching and George W. Truett Chair of Pastoral Ministry, Southwestern Baptist Theological Seminary

Occasionally God raises up a Nehemiah. He has quietly been preparing to lead a great work. Often these servants have a variety of experiences and have been faithful in development of both the understanding and the implementation to fulfill their calling. In Adam Hughes and Jody Dean, God has provided two Nehemiahs to provide a heart-and-head textbook to guide those responding to God's call. *Together We Lead* serves as a solid pathway forward.

—Dr. Tony Lambert,
Senior Pastor, Picayune First Baptist Church

Hughes and Dean have created a text for biblical leadership that engages the reader with extensive scriptural depth and engaging practical application. *Together We Lead* covers every ministry phase from calling to change to conflict and everything in between. I found myself reflecting on my ministry and what I might have done more efficiently and effectively had this book been available 40 years ago! I look forward to using this book to train current and future leaders for kingdom work in my church. Well done, Jody and Adam!

—Dr. Jimmy Stewart,
Senior Pastor, First Baptist Church Gulfport

TOGETHER
WE
LEAD

Integrating Church Leadership and
Administration for Ministry Success

Adam Hughes and Jody Dean

NEW HOPE®
PUBLISHERS
Imprint of Iron Stream Media
Birmingham, Alabama

Together We Lead: Integrating Church Leadership and Administration for Ministry Success

New Hope Publishers
100 Missionary Ridge
Birmingham, AL 35242
New Hope Publishers is an imprint of Iron Stream Media.
NewHopePublishers.com
IronStreamMedia.com

Library of Congress Control Number: 2021940370

ISBN: 978-1-56309-424-8 paperback
ISBN: 978-1-56309-425-5 ebook

1 2 3 4 5—25 24 23 22 21
Printed in the United States of America

From Jody

My family has always been my biggest fan over the years.
To my kids, Lydia and James:
Your dad loves you, and I'm grateful
for your willingness to understand the time I needed to
write.
To my wife, Emily,
who is the reason I am even able to contribute to a resource
like this
through her loving support and encouragement.

I am also thankful for a host of mentors who invested in my
life over the years
with conversations and experiences that furthered my walk
with Christ
and helped me fulfill the call on my life to serve the Lord
wherever he leads.

From Adam

This book is lovingly dedicated to my four children,
Ashyln, Kenlee, Alex, and Kate.
And with gratitude greater than can be expressed in words
to my wife, Holly, who is the love of my life, my best friend,
and my partner in ministry.

Contents

Acknowledgments

A book such as this one requires the support and help of many people.

I (Adam) am especially grateful for several people and the role each played in the completion of this project. Thank you to Holly Hughes, my wonderful wife, who encouraged me from the beginning to take on this task and supported me so that I had the time I needed to complete my writing. Thank you to Zach Miller for running down references and sources, especially during the editing process. Thank you also to Carol Lemke for the hours you spent editing each chapter before submission and the many conversations we had about the wording for certain sections and clarifying several of the leadership concepts I attempted to describe.

I (Jody) am grateful for my wife, Emily, who was gracious to listen, encourage, and understand the time and focus of this project. Thanks to Sara Robinson for taking the time to edit and consider my chapters as they relate to the church and audience of readers from the lens of church administration. Also, thanks to Dr. Waylon Bailey for taking the time to listen as I asked the critical question, "What does a person in the church need today for a book like this?" and responding with his years of wisdom from teaching seminary students and pastoring growing churches.

We would also like to thank the administration of New Orleans Baptist Theological Seminary (NOBTS). We especially appreciate Dr. Jamie Dew, Dr. Norris Grubbs, and

Acknowledgments

Dr. Bo Rice. Thank you for granting us a platform to teach these concepts, influence students, and be involved in the leadership and administration "conversation" in the local church. Thank you for encouraging us to write this work.

Also, thank you to the students of the Church Leadership and Administration course at NOBTS. We appreciate you letting us "test" these theories in the classroom before putting them down in writing. Thank you for your feedback and honest critiques along the way. Finally, thank you to all the pastors and staff of local churches. We appreciate your faithful kingdom work more than we could ever put into words. Thank you for the painstaking efforts you give daily to the work of leadership and administration in your roles for the sake of making disciples of the Lord Jesus Christ. May this work honor him and help you in your endeavors in some small way.

Chapter 1

Answering God's Call

"I'm going to Fort Worth for a couple of years to finish my master of divinity, and then I'm going to come back to Arkansas and pastor for the rest of my life." "Not only will I never live and serve in New Orleans, but I'm never coming back to the city even for a visit." These statements are only two examples of what may be called "famous last words" as it relates to my (Adam's) calling to ministry. As a matter of fact, over a decade has passed since I completed my master's degree. As I was nearing the end of my time at Southwestern Baptist Theological Seminary, my wife and I made a list of specific ministry desires. Not only did we write the list in such a way to describe our own preferences, but at the time we genuinely felt as though the list represented the details that God wanted for our lives, marriage, and family. However, few details on that list regarding the what or the where of ministry have matched, now nor at any other time since the list's composition, what we actually have done in ministry. If you can decipher the irony of the first two sentences of this chapter, my position on faculty at New Orleans Baptist Theological Seminary is both a case-in-point and a double whammy.

Why is a call often so difficult to discern? Why do so many people struggle to know specifically what they have been called to do? What do we mean by a "call to ministry"? More specifically, how do you know when you have been called and what you have been called to do? These are only some of the questions that have often permeated my experience and walk with the Lord for the last two decades. Although the specifics may be different, my guess is many who are reading this book can relate. If we believe we serve a God who has spoken, wants to use us in ministry, and does specifically call individuals into vocational ministry, then why is that which is described here so often the case?

As we examine scripture, there are several general statements we can make about the calling of God on an individual's life. For instance, we know every believer is called generally to a life committed to Christ, growth in discipleship, and service in the kingdom (1 Peter 1:13–21; Colossians 2:6–7; 3:12–17; Matthew 28:18–20; Acts 1:8). As it relates to the specific call of God, a monolithic or standard pattern does not seem to exist. However, example after example in both the Old Testament and New Testament indicate that when people were called by God to a specific task or for a specific purpose, they knew it. Moses's call was different from Isaiah's call, yet they both responded. Peter's call was different from Paul's, but they both followed Christ.

What have you answered the call to do? We can make three statements in reference to this question at this point. First, God's call is always relevant to the times (Isaiah 6:8–9). Second, God's call is always related to a people in that time (Acts 9:15–16; 20:28). And finally, the content of your call may take years to fully define and develop. Perhaps there are other questions we want answered. However, with these three axioms in mind, we must proceed knowing it is okay not to know all of the details of our call and to live with open hands before the Lord. Yet, at the same time, we must make several commitments regarding our call to serve.

In this chapter, we will explore the call to vocational ministry by examining Jesus's well-known command to his disciples to "take up [their] cross" in Matthew 16:24. The description of costly discipleship in this passage and its surrounding context will enable us to identify five characteristics of an authentic call—which then lead to five statements that clarify what a call is and will help someone who may be struggling to answer God's call. Although the chapter is designed with the vocational minister in mind, the content is general enough to be useful to anyone who has a desire to serve in the context of ministry leadership.

The Call to Serve

> From that time Jesus began to show His disciples that He must go to Jerusalem, and suffer many things from the elders and chief priests and scribes, and be killed, and be raised up on the third day. Peter took Him aside and began to rebuke Him, saying, "God forbid it, Lord! This shall never happen to You." But He turned and said to Peter, "Get behind Me, Satan! You are a stumbling block to Me; for you are not setting your mind on God's interests, but man's."
>
> Then Jesus said to His disciples, "If anyone wishes to come after Me, he must deny himself, and take up his cross and follow Me. For whoever wishes to save his life will lose it; but whoever loses his life for My sake will find it. For what will it profit a man if he gains the whole world and forfeits his soul? Or what will a man give in exchange for his soul? For the Son of Man is going to come in the glory of His father with His angels, and WILL THEN REPAY EVERY MAN ACCORDING TO HIS DEEDS.
>
> "Truly I say to you, there are some of those who are standing here who will not taste death until they see the Son of Man coming in His kingdom." (Matthew 16:21–28)

In this passage, we see five characteristics of an authentic call. To understand the passage's relationship to a call to serve God, the background of the text is not insignificant. From a thirty-thousand-foot view, Jesus's definition of and instruction on difficult or costly discipleship must be the lens through which these verses are understood.

The immediate context of this text is important. In verses 13–20, Matthew explained, "Now when Jesus came into the district of Caesarea Philippi, He was asking His disciples, 'Who do people say that the Son of Man is?' And they said, 'Some say John the Baptist; and others, Elijah; but still others, Jeremiah, or one of the prophets.' He said to them, 'But who do you say that I am?'" (Matthew 16:13–15). I have visited Caesarea Philippi on two occasions. This location is a unique site in the Holy Land. Near the back of the city, there is a cave located at the bottom of a large cliff. Inside this cave is a spring, and the spring is the source of a river that originates at the back of Caesarea Philippi. This river continues to flow through the middle of the remains of the city, and tourists on a pilgrimage can see it to this day.

In Jesus's day, the phrase "gates of Hades" was believed generally to represent and express the "powers of death."[1] Specifically, however, on top of a ledge next to the river and underneath the cliff in Caesarea Philippi were several temples to pagan gods. The most notorious and perhaps nefarious of these gods was Pan. Child sacrifice was included in the regular worship of Pan. In fact, Caesarea Philippi was so closely associated with and a center for the worship of this god that formerly the city was known as Paneas.[2] Ruins of these temples, and especially the temple of Pan, which stands the closest to the cave out of which the river of the city flows,

---

[1] Craig L. Blomberg, *Matthew*, The New American Commentary, vol. 22 (Nashville: Broadman Press, 1992), 253.
[2] Blomberg, 250.

are still visible. Interestingly enough, because of the popular belief then that the cave represented the power of death, was near the place of the gods, and was the crossing to the afterlife, it was referred to commonly as the "Gates of Hades." Historians explain that those who died there were often buried with coinage so that they could afford to be ferried to the life to come.

Caesarea Philippi is approximately twenty-five miles north of the Sea of Galilee. On a tour bus, this trip is not easy. One can only imagine how difficult it must have been by foot and how long the trip must have taken. Yet it is to this location, and I believe intentionally so, that Jesus took his disciples to ask, "Who do people say that the Son of Man is?" (v. 13). Why would he choose this out-of-the-way and somewhat difficult-to-reach location to ask this question? Perhaps there are several reasons, but ultimately the setting suggests this was the perfect location to teach the disciples a profound truth about the power of the gospel and a gospel calling.

So what does it look like to answer God's call? How can we know that we are answering God's call?

The Context Is the Service of the Gospel (vv. 21–23)

In verse 16 and in answer to Jesus's question, Peter made an accurate profession about the one whom he was following: "You are the Christ, the Son of the living God." In response, Jesus made perhaps an even more profound statement: "I also say to you that you are Peter, and upon this rock I will build My church; and the gates of Hades will not overpower it" (v. 18). More than a little debate has resulted in church history over the meaning of the designation "this rock."[3] However,

---

[3] The most likely possibilities for what Jesus meant by the designation "this rock" fall into three categories. The first possibility is Peter himself,

the meaning of "this rock" is not the most significant part of this passage as we consider a call to ministry. What is more important to consider here is the metaphor of the gates of Hades not prevailing and what these gates will not prevail over. We will take the latter first.

What will the gates of Hades not prevail over? The only two realistic options seem to be "this rock" or "My church." In Greek, all three words—*rock, church, it*—match in gender and number[4], so linguistically either option would work. However, *church* is the noun nearest in proximity to the pronoun in question. Normally, unless context does not allow, a pronoun is considered to refer to the closest noun that matches in gender and number. Therefore, the only sensible choice is that the church of Christ is that which the gates of Hades will not overpower. But what about the strange metaphor that gates will not prevail?

Normally gates are not considered offensive weapons. They are not that which overpower or overtake enemies. Quite the opposite. They usually protect against the enemy

---

in which Jesus is using a wordplay indicated by the similarity between Peter's name and the Greek word for *rock*. If this is what Jesus meant, perhaps it was foreshadowing Peter's role as the leader and founder of the Jerusalem church on the day of Pentecost (Acts 2). The second and third possibilities are closely related but distinct. Jesus may have been referring to the act of confessing that Jesus is the Christ, a profession for which Peter serves as the model. If this is the meaning, then the idea is that Jesus would build his church on the same confession of other believers throughout the ages. Finally, Jesus may have been referring to himself, the content of Peter's confession, as the rock. If this is the meaning, then the idea is that Jesus would build his church on the fact that he is the promised Messiah, the content of the gospel. This author takes the interpretation described in the third category, based on the context of what Jesus said next. For a more detailed discussion of what is meant by "this rock," see Blomberg, 251–54; and R. C. H. Lenski, *The Interpretation of St. Matthew's Gospel* (Minneapolis: Augsburg, 1964), 624–28.

[4] All three words are in the singular feminine form.

and keep invaders from overpowering or overtaking those residing behind the gates. This is the common use for us today, and it was the common understanding in Jesus's day as well. However, remember the setting and the unique characteristics of Caesarea Philippi. At the back of the city near a display of paganism representing lies, destruction, and religious hopelessness sat a cave known as the "Gates of Hades." I believe that Jesus was using this backdrop as an image—a metaphor—to represent all the satanic schemes in the world that will attempt to overpower the church, and her "calling" to proclaim the gospel of Jesus Christ is clear. And these gates will not win!

This is the context, then, that in verse 21 Jesus began to explain what it means for him to be "the Christ" and how it is that the gates of Hades will not overpower the church. Essentially, what he described is his death, the gospel of the Lord Jesus. "From that time Jesus began to show His disciples that He must go to Jerusalem, and suffer many things from the elders and chief priests and scribes, and be killed, and be raised up on the third day." And we remember Peter's response. He rebuked Jesus and made a bold declaration that he would not allow this action. What we must understand here is that Peter's rebuke was against what it meant for Jesus's statement to be true and what was necessary for even Peter's salvation. Jesus's answer and the position he espoused is striking: "But He turned and said to Peter, 'Get behind Me, Satan! You are a stumbling block to Me; for you are not setting your mind on God's interests, but man's'" (v. 23). According to Jesus, Peter was being the agent of Satan to prevent the ministry of Christ. To say it another way, he was working with the very gates that would not prevail against the church and thus the ministry to which Peter was called.

Why does this matter for us? In Peter's position and Jesus's counter, we see the first truth concerning an authentic call to ministry leadership. In order to answer the call, at a minimum, we must not work against the gospel. To put this in the positive, to answer the call we have to agree with the gospel.

The Call Is an Invitation to Follow a Person (v. 24)

In verse 24, the broader context of discipleship, or more generally a call to minister in Jesus's authority, is set. Jesus used the opportunity in Caesarea Philippi and the discussion of the gospel to transition into a definition or description of costly discipleship: "Then Jesus said to His disciples, 'If anyone wishes to come after Me, he must deny himself, and take up his cross and follow Me.'"

To understand the implications of what Jesus was calling his disciples to, a consideration of his terms may be helpful. Why did Jesus use two terms that seem synonymous in this call, and what significance is highlighted by the difference in these words? The word for *come after* holds the emphasis "to go on a course (presumably of someone specifically who had walked it before)."[5] The term for *follow* does carry the same meaning, generally, but with a slightly different nuance: "to move behind someone in the same direction" or "to follow or accompany someone who takes the lead."[6] Perhaps the truth Jesus intended is that if anyone wants to live like he has lived, walk like he has walked, do that which he has been seen doing, in other words, "come after me," then naturally this one must follow or walk closely behind *him*. Conceptually this makes sense. Jesus's statement is not complicated; it is logical.

---

[5] Walter Bauer, *A Greek-English Lexicon of the New Testament and Other Early Christian Literature*, ed. Frederick William Danker, 3rd ed. (Chicago: University of Chicago Press, 2000), 394. This lexicon will hereafter be referred to as BDAG (Bauer, Danker, Arndt, and Gingrich).
[6] BDAG, 36.

For understanding costly discipleship and the call to minister after Jesus, the object we are called to follow is significant. Notice the "who" of the call in verse 24. How does Jesus end his statement? We are not to pledge our allegiance to an idea. Our eyes do not look to a set of religious rites for hope and truth. Our model for life and ministry is not a philosophy or even a worldview. Instead, we look to a person. We are called to "come after" a person by "walking closely behind," in the steps of, this very same person. This person is clearly the Christ of the gospel, and he is the one who saves us and whom we proclaim. In order to answer the call, we must follow Jesus.

The Content Is a Command to Lose Your Life (v. 24)

A second detail from verse 24 is helpful for our understanding of an authentic call. An approach we could take to this passage is to examine each of the three phrases that Jesus used to describe discipleship individually and in detail. Word studies on *deny*, *take up*, and *follow* certainly yield some interesting and helpful results. However, for our purposes, these details may not be necessary. If we take Jesus's statement here more holistically and collectively, his simple and overt point becomes obvious. Furthermore, this process prevents us from missing the proverbial forest for the trees. Here is why this is the case. A derivative of this same statement is recorded five times in the Gospels. Other than the present location, it is also in Matthew 10:38; Mark 8:34; Luke 9:23; and Luke 14:27. More significantly, each of these four times the Gospel writers record Jesus using this statement, they do so, as Matthew does in chapter 16, in the context of Jesus teaching on serving him and serving like him. This, then, is Jesus's point: the costliness and the call to be worthy of discipleship.

9

The call and costliness of discipleship relates to how his original hearers would have taken the statement to "take up his cross." Today, we have sterilized this statement to make it safer for us. We often turn it into a metaphor that loosely means giving up preferences and desires to live a life serving Jesus and doing his will. This perspective may present an application of biblical truth for us, but there are at least two reasons why Jesus's audience would have understood his statement differently. First, the cross was not a metaphor for living the Christian life for them. The only referent, and thus meaning, that the cross had then was as a Roman execution device. Second, remember what Jesus had just taught his followers and the context in which he had taught them this truth. He is going to Jerusalem to die. Jesus was not going to die metaphorically to self; he was going to die literally on the cross.

Simply saying we are going to give up our own preferences or way of living does not capture the meaning of Jesus's call here. We are called to costly discipleship. We are called to be worthy of Jesus. We are called to, at least, be willing to lay down our lives. In order to answer the call, we must come and die. This is a difficult statement. We are called, then, potentially to give up so much if we answer the call to follow Jesus. Do we have any confidence in this calling? Is there any place to look for hope as we pursue his calling?

The Comfort Is a Promise that You Not Lose Your Soul (vv. 25–27)

Included in verses 25–27 are a series of *gar* clauses in Greek, usually rendered as "for" in most English translations. These clauses and their consecutive order are important because on most occasions this type of construction in the Greek

New Testament indicates that these are explanatory clauses.[7] The use of an explanatory clause "indicates that additional information is being given about what is being described."[8] Essentially, then, these three verses are giving reasons or providing grounds for why Jesus's disciples and, by way of application, we should have confidence to follow him even if this is a call to "come and die."

Therefore, included in these verses are three axioms that originally seem arbitrary and somewhat unrelated. Upon further examination, however, these statements are connected and are a part of an overall point of comfort that Jesus gave to those who would take up his call. First, Jesus explained that the only way to find real spiritual life is to lose one's desire to value his or her self and life over Jesus. A person must lose his or her life for Jesus (v. 25). Second, Jesus argued that a person's soul is his or her most prized possession. Losing one's soul to gain the world is a net loss (v. 26). Finally, the crux of the entire argument is found in verse 27, which is the third and final of the three consecutive *gar* clauses. Part of the significance of this verse is that it refers to three Old Testament passages. The statement that Jesus will come in the glory of his Father with his angels is probably an allusion to Zechariah 14:5. The quote "and will then repay every man according to his deeds" is recorded in both Psalm 62:12 and Proverbs 24:12. The emphasis Jesus was making is that he is equal with the God of the Old Testament and thus his authority over man, life, death, judgment, and reward is equal to God's as well.

Therefore, the final and ultimate grounds for why an individual can follow Christ even if the call is to "come and die" is because Jesus is the ultimate judge and life giver.

---

[7] Daniel B. Wallace, *Greek Grammar Beyond the Basics: An Exegetical Syntax of the New Testament* (Grand Rapids: Zondervan, 1996), 673.

[8] Wallace.

His coming to reward deeds is certain (Matthew 16:27). A disciple can follow Jesus and answer the call to die knowing that losing life for Jesus is the only way to find life, because a person's soul is his or her most important possession. And since Jesus is the one who holds authority over that soul, he holds the right to make the final judgment and offers the ultimate reward. In order to answer the call, we can have certainty that whatever we lose physically will be gained spiritually.

The Certainty Is the Guarantee of the Realized Kingdom of Christ (v. 28)

"Truly I say to you, there are some of those who are standing here who will not taste death until they see the Son of Man coming in His kingdom" (v. 28). The precise interpretation of this verse is somewhat difficult to determine. Perhaps the most relevant aspect to consider as we attempt to establish our conclusion is whether any of those standing there saw Jesus coming in his kingdom before their deaths. If we take Jesus to mean his second coming by the designation "coming in His kingdom," then answering this question and reconciling what Jesus said with what occurred is challenging if not impossible. Therefore, what did Jesus mean by this profound statement? The reasonable interpretation can be placed in two broad possibilities. First, he was referring to his parousia. However, he was doing so in a way that either took another event, such as the destruction of the Jerusalem Temple in AD 70 as a representation of God's judgment in Christ, or he intended his audience to be viewed in a wider sense, including all who would read the Gospels, us and those yet to come, until the future time of Jesus's return.[9] Second, he was simply referring to some other near event in his life

---

[9] Lenski, *Interpretation of St. Matthew's Gospel*, 648–49.

and ministry such as the transfiguration or the resurrection of which all, with the exception of Judas, witnessed before their deaths.[10]

When considering Matthew's Gospel more holistically, however, another and perhaps less specific option exists. Throughout his Gospel, Matthew seems to emphasize the "already" part of Jesus's kingdom. We do not have the space to parse out this idea completely, but the two places this seems clear is the birth narrative and the Sermon on the Mount. For instance, Matthew began his Gospel showing the fulfillment of prophesy proving that Jesus is the long-awaited King.[11] Furthermore, Jesus bookended the beatitudes with two statements indicating that a certain group *now* possesses the kingdom.[12] Matthew appears to be proclaiming, "You do not have to wait for another king; the one who was promised is here!" Furthermore, when the King arrives, so does his kingdom. If you do not have a kingdom, you cannot have a king. However, if you have a King, you must have a kingdom. Therefore, even though there may be a "not yet" to Jesus's kingdom, for those in whose heart the King is already ruling, the kingdom has come!

---

[10] Blomberg, *Matthew*, 261.

[11] In at least five ways in chapters 1 and 2, Matthew explicitly communicated that events around Jesus's birth were fulfillment of Old Testament prophecy that related to the coming Messiah or King. As a matter of fact, an argument can be made that Matthew was the first to join together intentionally two separate prophetic ideas, that of a future king and a coming Messiah, in one person, showing that Jesus alone definitively satisfied the prophecy. See Matthew 1:22–23 and 2:5–6, 14, 17–18, 22–23.

[12] See Matthew 5:3 ("Blessed are the poor in spirit, for theirs is the kingdom of heaven.") and Matthew 5:10 ("Blessed are those who have been persecuted for the sake of righteousness, for theirs is the kingdom of heaven."). All of the other beatitudes in the list indicate a future reality. Noticeably these two in verses 3 and 10 indicate a present reality involving the possession of the kingdom.

Whereas the precise interpretation of this verse may be somewhat difficult to establish, the theology and point in context Jesus was communicating is not. There is a guarantee that the literal kingdom of the King is coming. Moreover, we who trust and follow him will see it and actually work to help bring it about. Therefore, in order to answer the call, we must find hope and motivation in the coming kingdom of Jesus.

Conclusion

In calling his disciples, Jesus showed that following him was costly but in his hands. Answering God's call to follow Jesus is life altering, but it is worth it. For a moment, we will return to the original purpose of this chapter and some of our original questions. Why is a call so difficult to discern? Why do so many people struggle to know specifically what they have been called to do? What do we mean by a "call to ministry"? More specifically, how do you know when you have been called and what you have been called to do? And ultimately, what does an authentic call from God look like? We still may not be able to answer all of these questions with precision and certainty, but as we look at these five characteristics, we can make a few definitive statements about the nature of God's call.

First, if your call does not lead you to serve the gospel, you are not answering God's call. Second, if your call leads you away from looking like or obeying Jesus, you are not answering God's call. Third, if the decision for your call is made for your comfort and based on your plans, you are not answering God's call. Fourth, if your call does not give you peace and satisfaction in Christ, you are not answering God's call. Finally, if your call does not involve living in the kingdom now with an eye toward building the kingdom to come, you are not answering God's call. If your call does not match all five of these truths, whatever it may be and whomever it may be from, it is not an authentic call from God.

Case Study

You are on staff at Third Baptist Church in Somewhere, America. You just went through one of the most difficult six weeks in your personal life and ministry that you can remember. A couple of weeks ago, your mother-in-law succumbed to her long battle with a terminal illness. Your church has held numerous other funerals over this period, including a member who was the leading encourager in the congregation and another who was a significant giver and tither. Furthermore, one of your senior adult classes, full of some leading voices in your church, is currently upset with the youth ministry and wants to prevent the youth group from using the church bus for future trips. They have made the proposal that each group secure their own transportation that can only be sanctioned and used by the group it is designated for. You also find yourself more and more discouraged by the current division and state of affairs in your community and the country as a whole. On top of this, your daughter's dog recently died. You feel overwhelmed and are slipping into depression. You are beginning to ask, "Is it worth it?" and, "Why do I do what I do?"

Taking into consideration the truths and axioms of this chapter, write a description or plan regarding how you would process through, understand, maintain, or perhaps even refocus your call in light of your current situation and feelings. Be specific, and be sure to include support as to why you plan to respond this way. In other words, *why* are you committed to your call and *how* do you plan to maintain this commitment? What motivates you to respond the way you have chosen? You may supplement your answer with other information and sources, but be sure to include information from our study of Matthew 16:21–28.

Chapter 2

Leading in the Bible

Perhaps the two most profound and direct statements Jesus made regarding leadership are in Matthew 15:14 and Luke 22:25–26. In speaking of the Pharisees' inability to "lead" others because of their lack of understanding, Jesus said, "Let them alone; they are blind guides of the blind. And if a blind man guides a blind man, both will fall into a pit" (Matthew 15:14).[13] Although Jesus focused on the negative here, his statement implies that some qualifications or characteristics of leadership are necessary. In another account in the Gospel of Luke, while addressing a dispute among the disciples about who was the greatest, Jesus gave the following reminder and rebuke: "The kings of the Gentiles lord it over them. . . . But it is not this way with you, but the one who is the greatest among you must become like the youngest, and the leader like the servant" (Luke 22:25–26). Now certainly this event is not the only time in the Gospels that Jesus called his disciples to follow his example of serving,[14] but clearly here he is approaching what leadership does. Both of these—the

---

[13] A similar statement is found in Luke 6:39. For this chapter, the version recorded in Matthew 15 will be examined because the context, as brief as it may be, helps with the interpretation of the passage and thus allows for a more accurate application based on the original intent.

[14] See Matthew 20:25–28 and John 13:12–16.

person and practice of leading—must be included in a robust description of leadership.

So, formally, what is leadership? How should we understand it conceptually? Some common components and foundational ideas about what leadership is do seem to exist, but with each expert, a unique or different perspective is emphasized. In 1997, for example, Warren Bennis and Burt Nanus claimed knowledge of more than 850 unique definitions of leadership,[15] and at the time of this publication, that statistic is more than twenty years old. A cursory look at the books in my personal library confirms the diversity even in Christian leadership definitions. John Maxwell argued, "Leadership is influence. That's it. Nothing more; nothing less."[16] John MacArthur gave almost precisely the same definition; however, in context he focused more on the character of the one leading: "To put it simply, leadership is influence. The ideal leader is someone whose life and character motivate people to follow."[17] Henry Blackaby and Richard Blackaby, the spiritual leadership gurus, explained, "Spiritual leadership is moving people on to God's agenda."[18] We observe distinctions and unique emphases even among some consensus within these definitions, which are all under the general classification of "Christian leadership."

Finally, Aubrey Malphurs, in his work *Being Leaders*, offered a more comprehensive definition with a specific emphasis and broad application to several different avenues of Christian leadership. "Christian leadership is the process

---

[15] Warren Bennis and Burt Nanus, *Leaders: The Strategies for Taking Charge,* 2nd ed. (New York: HarperCollins, 1997), 4.

[16] John C. Maxwell, *Developing the Leader Within You* (Nashville: Thomas Nelson, 1993), 1.

[17] John MacArthur, *The Book on Leadership* (Nashville: Thomas Nelson, 2004), vi.

[18] Henry Blackaby and Richard Blackaby, *Spiritual Leadership: Moving People on to God's Agenda,* rev. ed. (Nashville: B&H Publishing, 2011).

whereby servants use their credibility and capability to influence people in a particular context to pursue their God-given direction."[19] A monolithic definition, especially of Christian leadership, then, may be impossible to locate. We can, however, move toward a helpful working definition for the purpose of better understanding ministry leadership specifically. Considering the definitions already discussed, one wonders at this point why a new definition of leadership is needed at all. Before we can answer that question, we must evaluate the ministry leadership of Jesus.

In this chapter, we will consider the leadership model of Jesus—the perfect leader. Both leadership character and leadership principles will be identified from his leadership practice. Next, two representative samples of leadership from the Old Testament and two representative samples of leadership from the New Testament will be compared and contrasted with the leadership of Jesus. You will be encouraged that although each of these figures is flawed and far from perfect, both the character (the person of leadership) and principles (the practice of leadership) for leadership found in Jesus's ministry are represented in the lives of these leaders. Finally, a working characterization of biblical leadership will be offered.

The Leadership Model of Jesus

What specifically can we learn about the skills necessary for leadership from Jesus's statement in Matthew 15:14: "And if a blind man guides a blind man, both will fall into a pit"? Jesus made this statement to his disciples about the Pharisees. Before making this statement, Jesus had been in a confrontation with the Pharisees regarding Jewish traditions

---

[19] Aubrey Malphurs, *Being Leaders: The Nature of Authentic Christian Leadership* (Grand Rapids: Baker Books, 2003), 10.

and customs, specifically regarding the ceremonial washing of hands before a meal. The Pharisees accused Jesus's followers of breaking the "tradition of the elders" by not washing before eating bread. Jesus responded to their accusation by showing that they did far worse. They transgressed the Law for the sake of tradition.

Jesus used the Old Testament expectations regarding the treatment and care of parents and the fifth commandment specifically to make his case. Then, in verses 8–9, he applied Isaiah 29:13 to show their ultimate spiritual condition and hypocrisy:

> THIS PEOPLE HONORS ME WITH THEIR LIPS,
> BUT THEIR HEART IS FAR AWAY FROM ME.
> BUT IN VAIN DO THEY WORSHIP ME,
> TEACHING AS DOCTRINES THE PRECEPTS OF MEN.

Finally, in front of the crowd, Jesus reversed an assumed spiritual truth. He did so by proclaiming that the spiritual state of a person is determined not by mere religious traditions or lack thereof but by the internal condition of the heart: "It is not what enters into the mouth that defiles the man, but what proceeds out of the mouth, this defiles the man" (Matthew 15:11). The Pharisees' response was expected and typical—they were offended. Then, almost defending their reaction, Jesus made a statement, which revealed their real problem. They could not be any other way but indignant because they could not "see." They had no spiritual sight; they could not understand the truth that Jesus had just revealed nor could they grasp spiritual reality. They were in a sense "blind."

Although not the direct point, Jesus taught something about biblical leadership in this passage by stating a negative. A person cannot be spiritually blind and be a leader. He or she must have spiritual sight. Specifically, a biblical leader must be able to understand spiritual truth and grasp the reality of righteousness to lead others. To say it another way, one cannot lead others to a place he or she has never been. More generally, from the details of this passage, the truth is leaders must have certain personal characteristics and possess some practical skills and ability to lead. The person of leadership matters.

What specifically can we learn about the act of leadership from Jesus's statement in Luke 22:25–26: "The kings of the Gentiles lord it over them. . . . But it is not this way with you, but the one who is the greatest among you must become like the youngest, and the leader like the servant"? To desire a position, to have power, and to have the place of honor is human nature. No different was it at times among the disciples. In Luke 22, one of those times had arisen with the followers of Jesus. "And there arose also a dispute among them as to which one of them was regarded to be greatest" (v. 24). In this context, Jesus made a statement regarding what true leadership is not and what true leadership does.

In responding to the dispute among the disciples and their attempts to obtain the highest position, Jesus offered some instruction regarding what Christian leadership must not be like—what this leadership must never do. Christian leaders must not follow the example that seemed so prevalent among the Gentile rulers by "lording it over" those they are called to lead. What does this mean? Even without knowing all the details, that Jesus did not intend this action to be understood as positive is clear. He was not complimenting these kings for their power and ability to make followers obey by sheer might. The word Jesus used here is *kurieuō*. This word is the verbal cognate of the noun most commonly translated "lord," and it literally means "to exercise authority" or "rule."[20] The

---

[20] BDAG, 576.

word was used often to communicate the idea of "dominate."[21] This is the meaning apparently intended here.

The picture of leadership that Jesus described is one that domineered followers, influenced by force and coercion, and essentially viewed others not as ones to be nurtured but as those to be used for the advancement of the leader. This is not what Christian leadership is or what a Christian leader does. Instead, Christian leadership values and nurtures followers for the sake of their good. In the second half of this passage, Jesus contrasted this domineering leadership with an opposing idea in order to provide a picture of what Christian leadership must be like—what this leadership does. The pervading idea seems to be that the leader must minimize self and instead hold a higher consideration for the ones he or she is leading, subjecting self to his or her followers, "but the one who is the greatest . . . must become like the youngest." In a culture that valued age for wisdom, the youngest was one who was humble, listened, and gave deference to others.

Jesus continued by arguing that "the leader [must become] like the servant." The word Jesus used for "servant" is *diakoneō*. This word is related closely to the office of deacon. One of the formal definitions is "to carry out official duties, minister,"[22] but here the word should be understood more holistically in terms of meeting needs and helping others. The definition that best bears this meaning may be either "wait on someone at [a] table" or "meet an immediate need, help."[23] These descriptions seem to capture Jesus's use in his instruction to the disciples. Jesus called his followers, Christian leaders, to be those who would wait on others and meet the needs of their followers. Leaders, then, have some

---

[21] BDAG, 576.
[22] BDAG, 229.
[23] BDAG, 229.

actions they must never do and certain actions they must always do as they lead. The practice of leading matters.

Although not using the same terminology, Malphurs argued that both the person (character) in leadership and the practice (ability) of leadership matter in ministry. He explained that a key component of leadership is credibility. "Christian leaders are servants with . . . credibility. . . . Credibility is critical to leadership because without it pastors, their people in general, and their boards in particular don't trust one another."[24] Do we see the need for and the example of credibility in both the leadership of Jesus and his instruction on leadership? Is there a "who he is" component to the ministry of Christ? Yes! Three necessary characteristics of leadership are discernable in Jesus's leadership. First, a leader must be genuinely relatable. Second, a leader must be noticeably honorable. Finally, a leader must be competently able.[25] Once again, as seen in the life and ministry of Jesus, the person of leadership matters.

Malphurs also wrote that a key component of leadership is capability. "What makes one a super leader and another an average leader? I believe that a major factor is what a leader brings to a church or parachurch ministry—his or her capabilities."[26] His description of what capabilities are may be helpful for our understanding as well. "Capabilities include spiritual and natural gifts, passion, temperament, knowledge, skills, and emotions. They are important because they position the leader to do something eternally significant for God and his kingdom, to have kingdom impact."[27] Do we see the need for and examples of capabilities in both

---

[24] Malphurs, *Being Leaders,* 10, 50.

[25] The content of chapter 4 will be based on defining, validating, and exploring in detail each of these characteristics as identified through the ministry of Jesus.

[26] Malphurs, 73.

[27] Malphurs, 74.

the leadership of Jesus and his instruction on leadership? Is there a "what he does" component in the ministry of Christ? Again, yes! In Jesus's ministry leadership, three primary principles of leadership are observable. The principles are: he had God's goal instead of simply a good goal; he valued people over production; and he never sacrificed the eternal for the temporal.[28] Without question, as seen in the life and ministry of Jesus, the practice of leadership matters.

Now having explored the who and what of leadership in the example of Jesus, we want to look for these same marks in the ministry of others. We'll take a look at representatives of leadership from both the Old Testament and the New Testament in light of the ministry and teaching of Jesus.

Old Testament Examples of Leadership

Moses. Perhaps the events in Exodus 14 as Pharaoh pursued Israel is where we see Moses at his best.

> Then Moses stretched out his hand over the sea; and the LORD swept the sea back by a strong east wind all night and turned the sea into dry land, so the waters were divided. The sons of Israel went through the midst of the sea on the dry land, and the waters were like a wall to them on their right hand and on their left. Then the Egyptians took up the pursuit, and all Pharaoh's horses, his chariots and his horsemen went in after them into the midst of the sea. At the morning watch, the LORD looked down on the army of the Egyptians through the pillar of fire and cloud and brought the army of the Egyptians into confusion. He caused their chariot wheels to swerve, and He made them drive with

---

[28] The content of chapter 6 will be based on defining, validating, and exploring in detail each of these principles as identified through the ministry of Jesus.

difficulty; so the Egyptians said, "Let us flee from Israel, for the LORD is fighting for them against the Egyptians." (vv. 21–25)

Moses's leadership was on full display as he led Israel out of Egypt. Although he had not arrived at it easily, here he acted in complete obedience and trust in the Lord. He was humble. He had overcome his past to capture his future. If he was ever decisive and sure, he seemed to be in this moment. Finally, he was a man of sacrifice.

Yet at the same time, Moses remained an extremely flawed individual. Three specific episodes, which reveal this fact, come to mind. His argument with God about his call to go back to Egypt (Exodus 4) showed at times he failed to see God's mission and missed an eternal perspective. Then, on his return trip to Egypt, his wife Zipporah had to intercede to prevent God from killing Moses because he had not been obedient and circumcised his sons. The event concluded with Zipporah calling Moses a "bridegroom of blood" (v. 25). All the nuances may not be clear, but it is obvious this saying was not intended as a compliment. Furthermore, it illustrates that Moses, on occasion, could be prone to have a less than honorable character. Finally, Moses showed a complete lack of wisdom and appropriate care for others by attempting to serve as the sole judge for all the people's cases and disputes after the Exodus. Perhaps all that stopped this madness was the intercession of his father-in-law, Jethro, and his wisdom regarding managing the people's future disputes (Exodus 18). At times, Moses lacked genuine relatability, competence, and did not always value people over production.

As imperfect as he may have been, however, Moses displayed one of the characteristics and two of the principles of Jesus's ministry. At the Red Sea, Moses showed his competence. He was a competently able leader. Furthermore, he acted under conviction regarding God's goal rather than simply a good goal, and he was unwilling to sacrifice the eternal for the temporal.

Joshua. Perhaps Joshua and his leadership are forever connected to, and thus synonymous with, two events. The first is when he led the children of Israel across the Jordan and into the Land of Promise.

> Then Joshua commanded the officers of the people, saying, "Pass through the midst of the camp and command the people, saying, 'Prepare provisions for yourselves, for within three days you are to cross this Jordan, to go in to possess the land which the LORD your God is giving you, to possess it.'" (Joshua 1:10–11)

The second is the clarion call he leaves with the people near the end of his life.

> Now, therefore, fear the LORD and serve Him in sincerity and truth; and put away the gods which your fathers served beyond the River and in Egypt, and serve the LORD. If it is disagreeable in your sight to serve the LORD, choose for yourselves today whom you will serve: whether the gods which your fathers served which were beyond the River, or the gods of the Amorites in whose land you are living; but as for me and my house, we will serve the LORD. (24:14–15)

On both occasions, several tremendous characteristics of Joshua, his ministry, and his leadership are on display, not least of which are his courage, faith, obedience, and ability to manage a crisis and transition. He faithfully served Moses for approximately forty years, and he was noted for his ability to give clear instruction and direction. To some degree, in the person of Joshua, each of the characteristics of Jesus's ministry are exhibited and each of the principles of Jesus's leadership are applied. Yet both of these events in Joshua's life provide further details, which point to some noticeable deficiencies in his leadership ability, confidence, and commitment.

In Joshua 1, while calling and charging him with the task of leading Israel into the Promised Land, the Lord had to command Joshua three times to be strong and courageous. This directive culminated with "Do not tremble or be dismayed, for the LORD your God is with you wherever you go" (v. 9). In addition, Joshua's charge to the Sons of Israel in chapter 24 concluded with Joshua stating his lack of confidence that they would indeed obey the Lord, a result that occurs one generation later. "Then Joshua the son of Nun, the servant of the LORD, died at the age of one hundred and ten. . . . All that generation also were gathered to their fathers; and there arose another generation after them who did not know the LORD, nor yet the work which He had done for Israel" (Judges 2:8, 10). What is missing conspicuously from this account is a mention of a great effort on the part of Joshua to prevent this future failure.

If the details surrounding the ministry of Moses and Joshua teach anything about leadership, it is that the person and practice of Jesus's leadership may be followed, but it cannot necessarily be perfected.

New Testament Examples of Leadership

Since we looked at one key leader in the Old Testament followed by his successor and one of his mentees, we will follow this same pattern in our overview of leadership in the New Testament. To begin, we'll look at one of the most prominent individuals in the New Testament who also happens to be one of the two most recognizable leaders in the church besides Christ himself—Saul of Tarsus, better known as the apostle Paul. Then, after examining Paul's leadership, we'll briefly examine the ministry of his most well-known protégé, Timothy.

Paul. Much could be written and discussed about Paul and his leadership. He was certainly bold, direct, and kept a single-minded focus on the mission of God in his life and ministry. These facts, as well as his accolades and training, are well known and established. However, perhaps to see the personal side of Paul's ministry and thus his character and principles in leadership, two passages should not be missed. The first passage under consideration was not written by Paul himself but does give the details of one significant event in his leadership.

At the end of his longest-tenured ministry in any single location, Paul prepared to depart from Ephesus. Luke described his emotional meeting with the elders in Acts 20:

> And now, behold, I know that all of you, among whom I went about preaching the kingdom, will no longer see my face. Therefore, I testify to you this day that I am innocent of the blood of all men. For I did not shrink from declaring to you the whole purpose of God. Be on guard for yourselves and for all the flock, among which the Holy Spirit has made you overseers, to shepherd the church of God which He purchased with His own blood. I know that after my departure savage wolves will come in among you, not sparing the flock; and from among your own selves men will arise, speaking perverse things, to draw away the disciples after them. Therefore be on the alert, remembering that night and day for a period of three years I did not cease to admonish each one with tears. And now I commend you to God and to the word of His grace, which is able to build you up and to give you the inheritance among all those who are sanctified. (vv. 25–32)

Who can deny Paul's character as a minister? He was honorable, and he was an able leader. How can anyone miss that his ministry was principled and gospel-driven? He had God's goal in mind. He certainly prioritized the eternal. Moreover, after reading how the narrative ends, who can question that he was genuinely relatable and valued people over production? "When he had said these things, he knelt down and prayed with them all. And they began to weep aloud and embraced Paul, and repeatedly kissed him, grieving especially over the word which he had spoken, that they would not see his face again. And they were accompanying him to the ship" (vv. 36–38).

For further confirmation of Paul's honorable character, relatable nature, care for people, and focus on God's mission and an eternal perspective, a look at a second, perhaps less obvious passage regarding his ministry is helpful.

> For we never came with flattering speech, as you know, nor with a pretext for greed—God is witness—nor did we seek glory from men, either from you or from others, even though as apostles of Christ we might have asserted our authority. But we proved to be gentle among you, as a nursing mother tenderly cares for her own children. Having so fond an affection for you, we were well-pleased to impart to you not only the gospel of God but also our own lives, because you had become very dear to us. (1 Thessalonians 2:5–8)

Of note is the fact that this passage was written by Paul's own hand as he reflected on his first trip to Thessalonica when he met and ministered among those who would become the Thessalonian church.

Yet, as with our previous examples, Paul did not always exemplify all of these qualities. Remember he described his own life and experience in relationship to God's standard as an ongoing struggle with sin (Romans 7:14–25).

Furthermore, his personal conflict with Mark, unwillingness to forgive, and thus absolute refusal to serve with him led to such a sharp disagreement with his missionary partner Barnabas that they broke up the team (Acts 15:36–41). These actions do not display an eternal perspective or commitment to God's goal. These are leadership flaws.

Timothy. Timothy was one of Paul's protégés. According to his words, Paul was Timothy's mentor. "The things which you have heard from me in the presence of many witnesses, entrust these to faithful men who will be able to teach others also" (2 Timothy 2:2). Therefore, examining an aspect or two of Timothy's leadership is only appropriate. Paul clearly had a lot of trust in Timothy. "As I urged you upon my departure for Macedonia, remain on at Ephesus" (1 Timothy 1:3). This trust included a belief in Timothy's character. "For I am mindful of the sincere faith within you, which first dwelt in your grandmother Lois and your mother Eunice, and I am sure that it is in you as well" (2 Timothy 1:5). Paul's high view of Timothy's ministry also included his abilities. "Do not neglect the spiritual gift within you, which was bestowed on you through prophetic utterance with the laying on of hands by the presbytery" (1 Timothy 4:14). Finally, this trust included Timothy's focus. "Guard, through the Holy Spirit who dwells in us, the treasure which has been entrusted to you" (2 Timothy 1:14).

Once more, however, Timothy was not perfect, and his leadership was not flawless. Otherwise, Paul would not have been compelled also to give Timothy warnings, reminders, and encouragement. "This command I entrust to you, Timothy, my son, in accordance with the prophecies previously made concerning you, that by them you fight the good fight, keeping faith and a good conscience, which some have rejected and suffered shipwreck in regard to their faith" (1 Timothy 1:18–19). We can fairly assume from this and other passages that Timothy struggled at times in ministry. "Let no one look down on your youthfulness, but rather in speech, conduct, love, faith and purity, show yourself an example of those who believe. Until I come, give attention to the public reading of Scripture, to exhortation and teaching" (1 Timothy 4:12–13).

Each representative from both the Old and New Testaments is flawed and far from perfect. However, collectively they serve as a living illustration that Christian leaders can and should emulate the example of Jesus in ministry. Furthermore, they serve as a reminder that both leadership character (the person of leadership) and principles (the practice of leadership) matter in ministry and should be focused on for effective service. These mutual realities should encourage leaders today. Although everyone has weaknesses and flaws and will be less than perfect and even fail at times, all ministers can achieve effective service and leadership.

After understanding Jesus's approach to and teaching on leadership and exploring how his leadership characteristics and principles can exist in imperfect people, this chapter will conclude by offering a working description of biblical leadership.

A Working Definition of Leadership

Back to our original question—if more than 850 definitions of leadership have been identified, why is a different approach and a new definition of leadership needed? There are at least two reasons. First, many approaches to Christian or biblical leadership seem too narrow to be helpful to everyone in ministry leadership but pastors. I have found this to be true even when a proponent of leadership gives a definition that seems to include more than only the office of pastor.[29] Our definition and approach will attempt to be broad enough to be helpful beyond the office of pastor only. On the other hand, others take an approach to leadership that may be too broad to be helpful to those desiring to be effective in ministry leadership. These authors take a pragmatic approach. They are willing to examine and offer any principle of leadership that "works," even those from the secular business world. This perspective is not wrong necessarily or unhelpful. The goal here, however, is to be narrow by design. Our approach will offer a distinctively biblical definition and thus aim toward, from theory to practice, a comprehensive biblical theology of leadership. This new definition and description, then, is needed and necessary because in it we are striving to be both narrow and broad—narrow enough to point to biblical leadership but broad enough to be helpful to anyone called to ministry leadership.

The perspective on Christian leadership, which follows, is foundational to all the subsequent leadership axioms in this book. Therefore, a brief explanation of each of the key components of the description will be offered after this definition:

> Biblical leadership includes the process of finding God's goal for a specific group of people, instilling that goal in them, equipping them to grow in Christlikeness and to fulfill the goal, and empowering them to serve God's eternal kingdom along with you.

---

[29] For instance, see Malphurs, *Being Leaders*, 49–71. Even though the author provided a definition that is inclusive of ministry positions beyond senior pastor, when discussing practical aspects of leadership such as credibility, he did so with a focus almost solely on the office of pastor.

Notice the designation *biblical leadership.* As argued previously, the definition is intended to be more specific than approaches to general leadership yet broader than ones that provide principles relating only to pastoral ministry. How the world defines a leader is not paramount in this approach. Our ultimate standard is not everything that "works" but rather is God's truth and authority in his Word. Accomplishing God's mission is the goal, and focusing on his purpose for leadership is paramount.

Likewise, a Christian organization's mission statement, which directs its functions and activities, or the ultimate purpose for which the ministry strives, should not be derived out of thin air. We do not have unlimited freedom here. God has already given the mission, and the biblical leader will always drive the people he or she serves toward that end. We pursue God's goal.

Additionally, a ministry leader's leadership is for and to a specific group of people. This perspective is imperative for a couple of reasons. First, in biblical leadership, people are the product. Second, logically and practically, one must have followers in order to be a leader. One part of this equation assumes the other. A Christian leader cares about the entire world, but he or she must know and remember who they serve in order to lead them. Moreover, a leader uses his or her influence to instill God's goal in the people he or she is leading.

Finally, the purpose and result of this type of leadership is unique. Ultimately the Great Commission of Jesus (Matthew 28:18–20) accomplished in and through followers is the ultimate goal of Christian leadership. First and foremost, discipleship—what is identified as Christlikeness in our definition—is the aim. Leaders want to see Christ formed in people. Then, through these people, the leader works to reach others and see Christ formed in them. Biblically, ministry leadership and disciple making are not intended to be a leader-only or leader-alone enterprise. Consider the implications of Paul's words to the Ephesians:

> And He gave some as apostles, and some as prophets, and some as evangelists, and some as pastors and teachers, for the equipping of the saints for the work of service, to the building up of the body of Christ; until we all attain to the unity of the faith, and of the knowledge of the Son of God, to a mature man, to the measure of the stature which belongs to the fullness of Christ. (Ephesians 4:11–13)

Leaders serve Christ by, and have the ultimate goal of, equipping and empowering followers to serve God's kingdom with them, leading to Christlikeness in others. This is biblical leadership.

Case Study

Back to Third Baptist Church in Somewhere, America. You have now worked through all of the "Is it worth it?" and "Why do I do what I do?" questions. Once more, you feel at peace and refreshed with your life at home, in the church, and in the community. Having been reminded of what a biblical calling is, you feel more convicted to lead and serve the people of Somewhere more than ever before. You are ready to reengage your ministry through your church. As you begin to do so, you recognize another problem. It had been there before, but because of all of the other challenges and personal struggles, you missed it. The church has become apathetic. The status quo is epitomized by a lack of attention to outreach. Any talk of the church's active involvement in ministries of eternal significance has ceased. Moreover, the vital signs of the church are trending in the wrong direction. Actually, attendance has been in a slow decline for the last ten years. Giving has taken a noticeable hit in the last eighteen months, resulting in the finance committee reducing the budget by suspending unnecessary spending with the plan to reimplement these budget items when things "turn around."

Understanding this reality, you want to begin to move the church forward. You are ready to begin to implement biblical leadership afresh, at least in your area of ministry. Before you can act, however, you know you need to settle your own philosophy of leadership because this philosophy will drive your leadership process. Using the information from this chapter, write a personal leadership philosophy that would serve as your guide and framework for both your character and practices as you plan and implement your leadership in the church. Here you are not looking for specific action steps. Instead, consider the biblical foundations, principles, and values that are paramount and would help maintain your focus on a distinctively Christian approach to leadership as you move into the action steps of your ministry. Be specific, and be sure to include support as to why you have arrived at this philosophy. You may supplement your answer with other information and sources, but be sure to include information from our study in chapter 2, especially the definition and description of biblical leadership.

Chapter 3

Leading the Church to Grow and Make Disciples

In this chapter, we explore the need to lead and administer disciple making so the church grows healthier and toward Christlikeness. Any given day, leadership errors and administrative mishaps can stop a ministry in its tracks. One mistake we certainly want to avoid is failure to implement a plan for discipling those under our leadership. Spiritual growth is the mechanism toward personal spiritual health and the main task in bringing God glory through making disciples in the local church.

As part of the leadership and administration processes of the church, there should be a clear pathway for believers toward spiritual maturity. Church leadership should consider whether the overall work of the church helps to multiply, reach, and develop disciples. "The church's ministries are its means or activities that God uses to implement or incarnate its marks of maturity in the believer's life. The ministry involves not only the activities (what we do) but the staff (who does it) and the budget (how much it costs to operate it)."[30]

---

[30] Aubrey Malphurs, *Strategic Disciple Making: A Practical Tool for Successful Ministry* (Grand Rapids: Baker Books, 2009), 87–88.

Sometimes we create processes that cultivate commitment to committees, meetings, and the work of the church but do not lead or manage strategies to enable a discipleship pathway for spiritual growth. When I take a good, introspective look at myself, I can be guilty of being detail-minded, but limiting my time investing in people for spiritual health through disciple making. Administrative structure and church facilities are essential; however, they are not the end game, only a framework through which we can work to lead and administer the work of the church.

If we aren't careful, we'll end up managing our ministries more than we lead. I like the way Tony Morgan explains this concept: "If strategies are the long-term view of how the vision gets accomplished, then systems are the day-to-day methods for executing the ministry strategy." He describes a healthy system as one that is simple, is replicable, and will "help people move from where they are to where God wants them to be."[31] Any given week may bring facility problems, meetings with staff, working through schedules, and handling financial challenges. It's common for a pastor to call and need help with administrative challenges or a committee chairperson to reach out, needing advice on resolving a church issue. No church is unique with the leadership and organizational challenges they face. Any church that has a facility and people will have weekly challenges as they strive to keep the vision and mission of the church in place.

The structure you adopt for how to govern the church should enhance and not limit disciple making. The frequency of committee or other leadership team meetings and how problems are navigated should all be carefully reviewed. From a biblical foundation, a church government philosophy that allows the most straightforward but healthiest path toward

---

[31] Tony Morgan, *The Unstuck Church: Equipping Churches to Experience Sustained Health* (Nashville: Thomas Nelson, 2017), 73.

unity and moves the church forward is crucial. Each church is different, and this process is one we cannot prescribe in a book for you, but later a few aspects of church guiding documents may help you process some of these areas of administration (see chapter 8).

When we approach discipleship, we should consider the administrative aspects to accomplish our strategy, program, or discipleship pathway. Curriculum, training, and facilities all have associated costs and a usage schedule that must be considered. Ministry volunteers require coaching and mentoring and create additional administrative aspects to leading the work. Everything a church desires to make, maintain, or accomplish is to use all those resources available to execute. When Jethro leaned into Moses about the work he was doing each day, he confronted the reality that Moses was carrying the burden of all the administrative tasks of the people.

Each church should consider the burden of work placed on ministers or leadership groups. We have to be guarded in ministry so as not to allow the full weight of the discipleship pathway to fall onto one volunteer or ministerial staff member. Unfortunately, over the years in ministry, I have observed faithful servants, both full-time ministers and volunteers, become so overburdened in the work that they simply walked away from the church. Some have, over time, returned to the church, but some have not returned to any church. Jesus modeled relationships over facilities and structures. Consider how Jesus poured into twelve that he chose from among the disciples. There were more disciples mentioned, but not all were enlisted into the core group of men Jesus called out, which is a crucial point for us to consider. We usually administer the work by merely inviting anyone interested to attend or serve. Often the pressures of ministry relegate us to accepting the available rather than choosing wisely. We should study and model Jesus's approach to disciple making to assure effectiveness.

Jesus modeled a targeted request from those who would follow. We know the work grew, and others followed too. Following the death of Christ, we know more than one hundred people were gathered together when Jesus appeared to them. A small group developed into a church that multiplied into other churches. Jesus's ministry strategy was significant as he worked through his chosen group of disciples. In the book of Acts, we then get to read of the growth and challenges that ensued after Jesus's resurrection and ascension. Still, many of us do not take the same administrative approach of starting small and developing a core group with growth and replication.

An organizational strategy that prioritizes discipleship, provides the space and resources necessary for growth, and focuses on connecting people to the church is crucial to having a reproducing model for discipleship. A century ago, leaders had administrative models for discipleship, Sunday school, outreach, church membership, and worship leadership. These discipleship models were restructured throughout the twentieth century, and many still exist among churches today. Your church may use GROW, D Groups, D Life, or another program that exists to help you create a disciple-making culture with the people in your church. An administrative model must function as the framework for discipleship and not become the end within itself for leadership development.

One example of a repetitive administrative framework is the quarterly curriculum for Bible study. Additionally, we should be careful that our church calendar doesn't look identical year to year. We are planning around our model for discipleship rather than allowing repetitive programs to endure endlessly. Before you shout "Amen" or stop reading, simply take a moment and reflect on your church administrative programs. Do they facilitate discipleship or foster needless repetition?

I tend to rely on the structure and process of canned church programs rather than keeping a pulse for the person being discipled. Flake's formula is an excellent example of a discipleship model that can be replicated by any church, regardless of size. Arthur Flake's formula was a standard process created in the early twentieth century for conducting a Sunday school for all ages each week in a local church.[32] Baptist Young People's Union also utilizes a straightforward process for developing students to walk with Christ. These strategies were not bad, and with a little work, they can be replicated and effective in advancing your organization and church. The programs have changed and new programs have developed over the years to have a process that guides weekly programming in the church for discipleship. Our challenge is to build a framework that prioritizes people and their spiritual growth over and above the aesthetics of a logo, name, or strategy. A few chapters later, we will discuss the concept of change in ministry. That information will be valuable to you if you realize a need to adapt church programs to advance the mission.

Paul and Barnabas had a great work together, but then a sharp disagreement caused them to take two different paths. Even amidst their separate work, they still made a significant impact in discipleship. Sometimes a ministry or church decides the best way to advance the mission is to do so as separate congregations or entities. In the work before us, we must be sure the programs and activities we develop and nurture collectively support a more extensive process that moves people toward Christ. Commit to reviewing the work consistently, whether weekly, monthly, or yearly, to see if the

---

[32] Arthur Flake, *Building A Standard Sunday School* (Nashville: Convention Press, 1922), 19.

plans provide an avenue for spiritual growth and personal evangelism. Paul and Barnabas's work did not stop due to difficulty; instead, it multiplied into two separate ministries.

The consideration to divide or begin other ministries deserves further consideration. Before you simply add churches, a church campus, or decide division is necessary to move forward, you should consider the source of the problem. The real issue could be hurt feelings or "turf issues" over someone's legacy or ministry, or a deeper problem that merits two ministries. Deciding to create new church campuses or ministries should not be an effort to keep pace with friends in ministry or neighboring churches. The church mission and vision should encourage your congregation to develop disciples through a clear pathway. Guard against the temptation of decision making for reasons that do not support your church mission and vision. Variety among sister congregations reflects the diversity of the body of Christ. The consumeristic church has emerged where people choose a faith community based on worship style, programming, and facilities. These should not be the driving factors in a disciple's life. The Holy Spirit should lead a person who walks with Jesus as to where they plant their family and to unite with a local body of believers.

As individual disciples, each of us should grow daily in our walk with Christ. Daily, spiritual growth is the primary way we develop as leaders. Those who serve in our ministries should model growth as disciples, not just hold a track record of service to the local church. You may have encountered a Sunday school teacher who responds to a new curriculum by letting you know she has been teaching longer than you have been alive. Or you may have experienced a business meeting where the words and actions of those in attendance leave you questioning the sincerity of their faith. The lack of personal, spiritual growth as a disciple can lead to unspiritual behaviors, which are often why other church members experience hurt and eventually leave the church. The letters of Paul to different churches affirm this reality. In writing to the church in Ephesus, Paul encouraged unity and maturity among believers, and in writing to the church at Colossae, he challenged them to be steadfast and conduct themselves wisely, which are examples of the challenges we have in keeping people maturing in the faith that each of us has within us. Still, in the end, the administration and structure of doing church business should reflect Christ and a commitment to personal spiritual growth through discipleship. If you experience something different, it may be time to reevaluate programs in light of the church mission and vision to ensure you are pointing the congregation toward Christ.

Church leaders should be known for their love of others. The burnout rate of volunteer leaders and paid staff in the church shows that many believe the work is too difficult or stressful and ultimately withdraw or leave over time. The stress factors for ministry are real, and the people of the church are not immune to the tragedy of burnout or overworking the schedule. You can go to the Barna group and assess whether you are nearing a risk of trouble in your ministry with burnout, relationships, or your spiritual development.[33] Conference after conference and church after church, I encounter people who simply state they are "hanging on by a thread." I wish this were not common, but it is certainly my experience. Realistically, we need to let people know they are loved and appreciated, specifically our ministry colleagues. Jesus said it this way: "I give you a new command: Love one another. Just as I have loved you, you are also to love one another. By this everyone will know that

---

[33] David Kinnaman, "Burnout & Breakdown: Barna's Risk Metric for Pastors," Barna: Pastors, January 26, 2017, www.barna.com/burnout-breakdown-barnas-risk-metric-pastors.

you are my disciples, if you love one another" (John 13:34–35 CSB). Church leaders should be growing disciples known for their love more than their work ethic or administrative prowess in the church.

Have you considered the costs? An attribute of growing disciples is "counting the cost" of ministry assignments. Anytime we prioritize the work of ministry over being a devoted disciple who makes disciples, then we have not considered the cost accurately. If our service to the church bears more weight than walking with Jesus, our priorities are conflated. Theologically, the gospel does not lead us to see a Jesus who ministered from a place of emptiness by being overly busy. We must model good stewardship of the gospel through our ministry positions, rather than a busy, overworked expression of the gospel. What does this look like practically? A family should experience regular dinners around a table together. People should experience conversations with an engaged listener. Life should communicate the rhythm of a disciple who regularly sits at Jesus's feet rather than one who believes he or she has to work for the favor of God. Most of us don't want to admit that we function like a Martha week in and week out based on our schedules. Jesus rebuked Martha's attitude and compelled everyone listening to consider the rhythm of Mary's heart instead. We as disciples cannot afford to busy ourselves like a Martha. When was the last time you withdrew from the crowds and craziness of a busy schedule to spend a devoted time in prayer? As leaders in the church, the tension between ministering to people and handling administrative details will always be a part of our weekly workflow. Remember to count the cost and prioritize spiritual growth over business and administrative tasks.

James writes about our efforts in being a disciple. We have to remember to be a person that follows Christ even during the challenges and struggles. James shares with us at the beginning of chapter 1 that we will face trials as we move forward as a disciple. Pause and read James 1, and then continue reading this chapter.

James notes the importance of remaining steadfast in our faith. We will mature in the faith as we remain committed to Jesus Christ. As you lead, you may find yourself struggling with an administrative aspect of the work or navigating change toward being more efficient in reaching and making disciples. James 1:5 instructs us to ask God if we lack wisdom. Obedience to God's Word will require you to pause and seek wisdom from the one who freely gives us what we need.

The biggest challenge in this chapter from James is not the testing of our faith but the obedience to follow the Lord. A rhythm for this pursuit is outlined for us in verse 19 and 20: "Be quick to hear, slow to speak, slow to anger; for the anger of man does not produce the righteousness of God" (ESV). We have to submit ourselves daily to this rhythm in our lives that moves each of us toward action. This action is described in verse 22, where James writes to become "doers of the word, and not hearers only, deceiving yourselves" (ESV). Maturing followers of Christ exhibit a lifestyle that reflects verbal claims of discipleship to Jesus. A few verses later, James further expounds upon the lifestyle of a true disciple: "Religion that is pure and undefiled before God the Father is this: to visit orphans and widows in their affliction, and to keep oneself unstained from the world" (v. 27 ESV).

A few questions for you as we move forward: What is hindering your walk with the Lord? Would others easily identify you as a disciple of Jesus Christ by the lifestyle you lead? Are you struggling to follow the Word of God in any area of your life? Do you listen well? You may need to ask your family and team members whether you listen effectively. Do you always have a quick answer, or do you pace your responses? Do you live life so pressed to achieve goals that you are always on the verge of coming across to others as being angry? James 1 helps us establish a biblical vision for discipleship in our ministries.

James wrote to remind us that the struggle is real, we will be tested, and our rhythms of being a person who walks with Christ can be challenging. Discipleship must not be thought of as an administrative process or activity. Our goal for discipleship should be a balanced approach between administrative details and the personal growth of those under our leadership. I encounter a lot of people who struggle with the balance. Those who lack an executive gift set become bogged down in the details, becoming overwhelmed week in and week out. On the other hand, those who are strong administratively may grow increasingly committed to details, forgetting that discipleship is about personal, spiritual growth. Discipleship administration could be one way you begin to gently shift your thinking about the details so you recognize that the significance of your ministry lies in the lives of those you lead.

Administrative oversight is necessary to achieve the mission or purpose of any ministry. Discipleship requires some administrative management to keep a pulse of the process and be sure that the purpose of discipleship is more significant than the administrative function of the budget, facilities, and human resources. The ministry struggle is real! Managing the volunteers for each ministry, ensuring operating capital to pay the bills, and managing facilities are necessary parts of leading a thriving church. However, in all the details, sometimes we unintentionally allow our weeks to become crowded beyond our ability to share the gospel faithfully with lost people. Beyond living an evangelistic lifestyle, we forsake the strategic investment into a few lives, as Jesus modeled for us. Administrative oversight helps us build and sustain healthier ministries that extend beyond our lifetime.

Discipleship is a commitment to guarding our time and prioritizing the art of disciple making. Over the years, I have observed people who are willing to serve in the church but who are not as interested in the discipleship aspects of ministry. Sometimes ministers are the ones who model being administratively busy for God yet are not as engaged in making disciples. The ebb and flow of ministry life will have busy seasons, families who come and go, and the inevitable highs and lows of serving people. When we stand before God, I pray our testimony is to join his mission in making disciples to reach all nations. Will your legacy be one of disciple making?

Tips for Becoming a Disciple Leader

1. Prioritize disciple making—schedule time to disciple others as a part of your weekly workflow.

2. Commit to modeling disciple making. People will follow your leadership.

3. Mentor other leaders in discipleship. Invite them to serve alongside you and learn the art of disciple making.

4. Strive for balance. Personal discipleship and administrative responsibilities can coexist. Be sure the churn of organizational management and weekly details do not limit intentional disciple making.

Questions for Self-Reflection

1. What model do you use for discipleship? Do you prefer a small group approach of less than twelve or an accountability group of less than five? Committing

to a process for disciple making enhances our spiritual commitment and development.

2. To whom are you accountable? Do you have people who help you stay focused on making disciples? List them.

3. How do you measure your discipleship progress? What is your assessment process in evaluating your approach to making disciples? Ministry leadership should prioritize making disciples through demonstration and modeling.

If you're new to disciple making, family is a great starting place. For the past several years, as I speak at conferences, equip lay leaders in the church, and teach seminary classes, I challenge those under my leadership to ask a simple question: Would you say the primary discipleship influence in your life was a parent? Without exception, the response is generally less than 20 percent of those in attendance. Parents are not prioritizing discipleship in their homes.

The home should be a foundational part of our disciple-making approach. As leaders, our discipleship process begins with those in our own homes. We are to be the front line for the spiritual formation in our families. We look out for their physical and emotional well-being. We strive each day to provide food, shelter, and other primary needs. Spiritual development should be a focus that carries more weight than providing food on our tables. In ministry, the focus of making disciples and having a pathway for discipleship is more important than our buildings, programs, and budgets. Administrative leadership must be done with excellence and not overlooked. Still, our ministry focus must be our corporate worship of the one true God and our priority of reaching and making disciples.

A pastor friend of mine was called to a church on the Louisiana bayou to serve and make disciples. The church had great hopes that he would help it stop its decade-plus decline and bring it into the new era of reaching families and making a difference in their community. A stated priority of the church was to have a discipleship pathway to reach children, youth, and adults. The people had developed great excitement in looking at every ministry and process with a new vision and strategy. They desired to achieve Christ's mission for the Great Commission until that meant they would have to change.

The steps were small, and the tweaks more cosmetic, but oh, did the people get testy! The first apparent signs were when people did not like the few tweaks to the stage and worship guide of "their" church. As they moved toward ministry alignment with a clear discipleship pathway, additional programs and schedules emerged and met a church with an unwillingness to change. Some church members got caught up with the program or how the ministries were labeled; others were upset over the Bible-study curriculum. Some were simply disgruntled as though they were experiencing a *Who Moved My [Church] Cheese* moment.[34] As time moved on, people grew more unified in making disciples, but the administrative process to shift the programs, schedule, and leaders to have a clear pathway is always going to be fluid. If one area grows, then space usage might have to change. If a ministry grows, the budget needs to be increased to provide appropriate resources. If a discipleship pathway works and the church grows, then additional funds, space, and staff leaders are necessary to keep the people moving on the journey. We can never solve the administrative process of making disciples. Still, we can become more efficient in

---

[34] Spencer Johnson, *Who Moved My Cheese: An A-Mazing Way to Deal with Change in Your Work and in Your Life* (New York: Penguin, 1998).

our administration so we do not distract from the mission to reach mature disciples in the faith.

Questions for Reflection

1. What aspects of your ministry need to be tweaked or changed to move the church toward a clear discipleship pathway?

2. What adjustments need to be made to allocate resources with budget, space, and leadership to be more efficient in making disciples?

3. What are you doing well as a ministry to make disciples?

4. What areas do you feel you are mature in your leadership and faith?

Chapter 4

Gaining Traction to Lead

Leadership is both who you are *and* what you do. In order to lead effectively, the leader's actions must display consistent and proficient patterns, but the leader, as a person, must also possess certain personal qualities. To lead, then, a person must, yes, be trusted to accomplish specific tasks, but first he or she simply must be *trusted*. This characteristic of trustworthiness is what James Kouzes and Barry Posner referred to as the "first law of leadership." They argued, "If you don't believe in the messenger, you won't believe the message."[35]

Consider the following. You may think another individual is the most competent communicator in the world but still not want him or her to serve as your primary Bible teacher or really to have any spiritual influence over you at all because you do not believe him or her to be a committed Christ follower. Therefore, in order to be a person others follow, a leader must possess specific biblical characteristics. In chapter 2, both the person and practice of leading

---

[35] James M. Kouzes and Barry Z. Posner, "Seven Lessons for Leading the Voyage to the Future," in *The Leader of the Future: New Visions, Strategies, and Practices for the Next Era*, eds. Frances Hesselbein, Marshall Goldsmith, and Richard Beckhard (San Francisco: Jossey–Bass, 1996), 103.

were identified. In this chapter, we will focus on the necessary characteristics of a leader, those which constitute the person of leadership and are foundational for effective ministry leadership.

The idea that the person of leadership (who the leader is) matters and is paramount in the ability of that person to influence followers and accomplish tasks in biblical leadership seems obvious. As noted previously, Malphurs argued that one key component of leadership is credibility. "Christian leaders are servants with . . . credibility. . . . Credibility is critical to leadership because without it pastors, their people in general, and their boards in particular don't trust one another."[36] Although there are clear differences from Malphurs's argument and the approach here, his description does affirm a couple of principles that support the focus of this chapter. Trust is critical to leadership. Leadership trust, and thus leadership holistically, is impacted not only by what a leader does and how he or she does it, but also in who he or she is.

Do we see the person of leadership in both the ministry of Jesus and his instruction on leadership? Is there a "who he is" component in the ministry of Christ? The answer to both questions is yes. At least three necessary characteristics of leadership can be found in the life of Christ as described in the Gospel accounts: first, a leader must be genuinely relatable; second, a leader must be noticeably honorable; finally, a leader must be competently able. In this chapter, we will explore these characteristics in detail. In order to do so, the three New Testament passages in which the biblical qualifications of a pastor are listed, 1 Timothy 3:1–7; Titus 1:5–9; and 1 Peter 5:1–5, will be examined. The same necessary characteristics that are present in the life and leadership of

---

[36] Aubrey Malphurs, *Being Leaders: The Nature of Authentic Christian Leadership* (Grand Rapids: Baker Books, 2003), 10, 50.

Jesus are required for the office of pastor in these passages. Although each passage's context relates to the office of pastor, three prerequisites will be discovered that are necessary for any minister to possess in order to be an effective leader. We will begin by examining these characteristics in the life and ministry of Jesus.

The Three Necessary Characteristics of Leadership in the Example of Jesus

Jesus Was Genuinely Relatable

Several passages in the Gospels illustrate our Lord's tremendous care for and relationships with people. In fact, it is difficult to look at the life of Christ and think about or describe what we read apart from his interaction with and concern for others. For the sake of space, however, the discussion will be limited to two such passages here. The first of these is Mark's description of Jesus choosing and commissioning his twelve disciples.

> And He went up on the mountain and summoned those whom He Himself wanted, and they came to Him. And He appointed twelve, so that they would be with Him and that He could send them out to preach, and to have authority to cast out the demons. And He appointed the twelve: Simon (to whom He gave the name Peter), and James, the son of Zebedee, and John the brother of James (to them He gave the name Boanerges, which means "Sons of Thunder"); and Andrew, and Philip, and Bartholomew, and Matthew, and Thomas, and James the son of Alphaeus, and Thaddaeus, and Simon the Zealot; and Judas Iscariot, who betrayed Him. (Mark 3:13–19)

At least two details of this passage are helpful.[37] One is that Mark limited the number of purposes Jesus had for calling and commissioning the twelve precisely to two. In verse 14, Mark explicitly told the two reasons: "And He appointed twelve, *so that* . . ."[38] The first reason is obvious. It is ministerial, evangelistic, if you will: "He could send them out to preach." In other words, Jesus picked them to help him accomplish his mission. However, the second reason, which Mark listed first, may be somewhat surprising. "So that they would be with Him." This seems to have nothing to do with the mission. It is relational. Therefore, of all the reasons Mark could give to describe Jesus's purpose for calling the twelve, the two he chose were to have help with the mission and to have others with him. The second detail is that the names of the twelve individuals are given in this passage. Sometimes the apostles are referred to collectively in the Gospels. Often we read the designation "the twelve." Not here however. Names are important. Names are intimate. Names uniquely identify and imply relationship. The names of the twelve have

---

[37] The descriptions and examinations of the passages in this chapter are not intended to be full interpretations of the texts in question. Space does not allow for such an approach. I am not intending to communicate that in every instance, my applications are the main thrusts or points of the passages in context. The use of each text primarily is intended to serve as examples of the leadership characteristics being described. However, at the same time, care has been taken not to take passages out of context in order to affirm position or make points that the texts will not support. At all times, practices that are consistent with solid contextual exegesis have been employed and, where appropriate and helpful, biblical language principles are applied and described.

[38] Italics added for emphasis. In the Greek text, verse 14 contains a *hina* clause. The most likely function of this clause in context is to indicate purpose. See Daniel B. Wallace, *Greek Grammar Beyond the Basics: An Exegetical Syntax of the New Testament* (Grand Rapids: Zondervan, 1996), 676–77. According to Wallace, a purpose clause "indicates the goal or aim of an action" (676).

not been lost in history to believers today. Mark knew and gave the names. Mark knew them because Jesus knew them. Jesus knew their names because they mattered to him.

The second passage to consider is from Jesus's instruction rather than from his example. The text in question is Luke 10:38–42. In the middle of Luke's Gospel, we read the now famous account of Jesus taking time to share a meal at the home of two sisters.[39] This act in and of itself signifies the importance of the relationship and the relational context of Jesus's ministry. However, when the passage itself is examined, a more specific emphasis emerges.

> Now as they were traveling along, He entered a village; and a woman named Martha welcomed Him into her home. She had a sister called Mary, who was seated at the Lord's feet, listening to His word. But Martha was distracted with all her preparations; and she came up to Him and said, "Lord, do You not care that my sister has left me to do all the serving alone? Then tell her to help me." But the Lord answered and said to her, "Martha, Martha, you are worried and bothered about so many things; but only one thing is necessary, for Mary has chosen the good part, which shall not be taken away from her." (Luke 10:38–42)

In this account, the application to the importance of relationships for Jesus may be more obvious than in the previous example.

This passage is not about lack of productivity or the evils of being task-oriented as a believer. If anything, the text displays the shortsightedness of being task-oriented to the detriment of relationships, especially a relationship with

---

[39] From other Gospel accounts, we know that these sisters had a brother named Lazarus, that Jesus had a previous relationship with them, and that he cared for them deeply. (See John 11:1–44.)

Jesus. For our purposes here, however, notice the comparison between the two sisters, the difference in their activities when Jesus was in the house, and the assessment Jesus made of those actions. First, in this passage Mary is identified and distinguished from her sister by her proximity, both physically and relationally, to Jesus. No other description of her is given. Martha, on the other hand, is identified by her distance, both physically and mentally, from Jesus. She was "distracted."[40] Second, the only action attributed to Mary in the text is one that emphasizes her relationship to Jesus. She was listening, and more specifically she was listening to Jesus and his word. In comparison, Martha is described as "doing" in this context. Interestingly, no object was referenced in the description of her activities. She simply was said to be making preparations. Preparation for what? Preparations for whom? We can guess, but Luke does not say. She was task-oriented with no apparent understanding of who the task was for and therefore why the task mattered.

Finally, the commentary Jesus offered regarding both sisters' behavior in the house is noteworthy. Notice the value he placed on each. First, he said Martha was "worried and bothered about so many things." Perhaps Jesus was intentionally highlighting a spiritual reality in Martha's life with the use of these two terms. However more than this, the major emphasis appears to be the many things she had chosen in contrast to the one she had neglected. Again, she was task-oriented. Perhaps this is the first recorded case of multitasking. On the other hand, Jesus's evaluation of Mary simply was that she "has chosen the good part." Jesus was not

---

[40] The word that is used here is *perispáo*, which may be better translated as worried, or "overburdened." See BDAG, 804. In fact, three terms are used in this passage to describe Martha and her activities that generally indicate that she was anxious or afraid. Perhaps these terms are intended to be synonymous to emphasize Martha's spiritual distraction and thus juxtaposing her spiritual "fear" with her sister Mary's faith.

devaluing Martha by his response. Instead, Jesus's evaluation points to the value of Martha and the desire that he had for her to understand the importance of a relationship, which in the moment she had missed. Yes, Jesus valued relationships. Ultimately, he emphasized an eternal relationship with him over everything else in this life, for he said it is the "good part" to be chosen. Jesus as a ministry leader, but also as the Savior, was genuinely relatable.

Jesus Was Noticeably Honorable

The Gospel accounts, and the New Testament as a whole, are wrought with examples and expressions of Jesus's honorable nature. In Luke 3:21–22, a brief but profound account of his baptism is recorded. "Now when all the people were baptized, Jesus was also baptized, and while He was praying, heaven was opened, and the Holy Spirit descended upon Him in bodily form like a dove, and a voice came out of heaven, 'You are My beloved Son, *in You I am well-pleased*'" (emphasis added). Furthermore, in the book of Hebrews, the following description of his nature as a whole is given: "For we do not have a high priest who cannot sympathize with our weaknesses, but One who has been tempted in all things as we are, yet without sin" (4:15). Perhaps then, to think about both the beginning of the public ministry of Christ and his accomplishment on the cross outside of the context of his high character and sinless nature is impossible. Once more, for the sake of space, I will limit the discussion here to two passages, which describe these attributes of Christ.

The first passage is Mark 14–15. The setting of this passage is the eve of Jesus's crucifixion and the night of his arrest and trials. At least two seemingly contradictory if not impossible conditions had to exist for Jesus to have accomplished the work necessary for our salvation. The latter, or the one more readily recognized, will be examined first. He had to die, and more specifically, he had to die on the cross. Second, he had to be innocent. More specifically, his innocence had to be sure. Why? Because the existence of either one of these conditions absent of the other would not have resulted in salvation. If, for instance, Christ had been declared innocent yet had not died on the cross, which would have been a normal outcome, man would have no salvation because no sacrifice would have been offered. If, on the other hand, he had been found guilty legitimately and then executed on the cross, which would have been common, man still would have no salvation because a righteous substitution would not have been given. When one has his own sins to die for, he cannot die for the sins of another. This truth leads to the details of the passage in question.

In context, Mark painstakingly showed that both conditions were met in Christ. Specifically, chapters 14 and 15, in preparation for the crucifixion, illustrate and emphasize not only Jesus's innocence but the statement by his enemies of said innocence. "Now the chief priests and the whole Council kept trying to obtain testimony against Jesus to put Him to death, and they were not finding any" (14:55). "Answering again, Pilate said to them, 'Then what shall I do with Him whom you call the King of the Jews?' They shouted back, 'Crucify Him!' But Pilate said to them, 'Why, what evil has He done?'" (15:12–14). "*Wishing to satisfy the crowd*, Pilate released Barabbas for them, and after having Jesus scourged, he handed Him over to be crucified" (15:15, emphasis added). On no less than three occasions, then, Jesus was declared righteous. These declarations are significant not only in terms of redemption but also in terms of understanding leadership. Jesus in his ministry's mission and leadership was noticeably honorable.

Not only did Jesus display this type of honorability in his life and ministry, and that at his toughest hour, but he called others to this standard as well. In Matthew 5:33–37, Jesus taught his followers about the need for integrity for those who are residents of the kingdom:

> Again, you have heard that the ancients were told, "YOU SHALL NOT MAKE FALSE VOWS, BUT SHALL FULFILL YOUR VOWS TO THE LORD." But I say to you, make no oath at all, either by heaven, for it is the throne of God, or by the earth, for it is the footstool of His feet, or by Jerusalem, for it is THE CITY OF THE GREAT KING. Nor shall you make an oath by your head, for you cannot make one hair white or black. But let your statement be, "Yes, yes" *or* "No, no"; anything beyond these is of evil.

The broader teaching was aimed at the practice of the Pharisees, who tried to obligate hearers to accept their lies as truth by attaching oaths to their statements that appeared close enough to God to be believed but far enough from him to not be the transgression of the Law. Even though the context of Jesus's statement here was more than likely a rebuke against this practice and the ones practicing it, at least one implication for us is that in ministry one's word should stand on its own. "But let your statement be, 'Yes, yes' *or* 'No, no.'" A believer should do what he says and keep what he promises. He should be a person of integrity. What is true of the believer generally must be true of the Christian leader specifically. Jesus was noticeably honorable.

Jesus Was Competently Able

The tendency may be to think or even say, "Well of course he was!" He was the divine Son of God, God himself in the flesh. He could not have been anything less. True as this may be, this perspective fails to consider two truths. First, Jesus was also 100 percent man. Therefore, the logic displayed in this viewpoint minimizes Jesus's humanity. Second, the fact that Jesus was divine, perfect, and endowed with the Holy Spirit of

God in a unique way does not mean that Jesus does not offer an example that can and should be followed. Recall Christ's words in the context of serving his disciples by washing their feet. "For I gave you an example that you also should do as I did to you" (John 13:15).

With this in mind, the context and content of Matthew 7:28–29 is worthy of consideration. The context is the conclusion of the Sermon on the Mount. This portion of the text may even be considered the response to Jesus's invitation. Perhaps what is contained in Matthew 5–7 is not only the greatest sermon of all time but also one of the most spectacular pieces of literature as well.[41] How perfectly needed and addressed was each subject; how understandable his communication; how vivid and illuminating his illustrations were; and finally how perfectly precise his applications are even for life today. Jesus was indeed the master teacher-preacher. William Barclay, in his introduction to *The Beatitudes and the Lord's Prayer for Everyman* espoused this position by aptly stating, "In this case the findings of the New Testament scholarship have confirmed that which the ordinary person instinctively feels. The detailed study of the Sermon on the Mount confirms the conviction that it is indeed the central document of the Christian faith."[42] Later he concluded:

---

[41] See Craig L. Blomberg, *Matthew*, The New American Commentary, vol. 22 (Nashville: Broadman Press, 1992), 93–96. In his introduction to the Sermon on the Mount, Blomberg summarized this position succinctly when he wrote, "Perhaps no other religious discourse in the history of humanity has attracted the attention which has been devoted to the Sermon on the Mount. Philosophers and activists from many non-Christian perspectives who have refused to worship Jesus nevertheless have admired his ethic." (93).

[42] William Barclay, *The Beatitudes and The Lord's Prayer for Everyman* (New York: Harper and Row, 1964), 11.

Therefore in what follows we are to see, not simply a statement made by Jesus on one occasion, but the substance of all that he habitually and repeatedly taught his disciples. We are not to see here only one sermon; we are to see the summary of the teaching which Jesus continually and consistently gave to his disciples. It is therefore nothing more than the actual fact to say that the Sermon on the Mount is the essence of the teaching of Jesus.[43]

Nothing less than the same opinion from those that he had called and were following him two thousand years ago would be expected. Yet, in a somewhat surprising turn of events, notice how the description of this discourse ends. "When Jesus had finished these words, the crowds were amazed at His teaching; for He was teaching them as one having authority, and not as their scribes" (Matthew 7:28–29). At the end of his sermon, not only did his followers recognize his skill, but the crowds did as well. Everyone who was around Jesus saw his profound and unique ability. Yes, Jesus was competently able. He accomplished his tasks with excellence. His ability to perform tasks and lead others in ministry was palatable and noticeable. We as leaders are called to follow the pattern of the Master.

The Three Necessary Characteristics of Leadership in New Testament Lists

As we consider the pattern of the three characteristics of leadership in the person and ministry of Christ, let us reflect on the following statement, which emphasizes our responsibility to consider the example of Christ in our ministries: *Failure in ability to imitate perfectly does not excuse failure in willingness*

---

[43] Barclay, 14.

to follow passionately. A leader is called to follow the pattern of Christ and strive to reflect Christ's character in his and her life and leadership. This command cannot be missed in the content of three New Testament passages, which give the biblical qualifications of a pastor: 1 Timothy 3:1–7; Titus 1:5–9; and 1 Peter 5:1–5.[44] Although each context specifically relates to the office of pastor, the qualifications can be helpful for any ministry leader for enhancing influence and gaining traction in a ministry setting.

A Leader Must Be Genuinely Relatable

That Jesus valued relationships and exhorted his followers to do the same has been well established. The qualifications for the office of pastor in the New Testament, and by association the encouragement for any ministry leader, displays the same emphasis.

> Therefore, I exhort the elders among you, as your fellow elder and witness of the sufferings of Christ, and a partaker also of the glory that is to be revealed, shepherd the flock of God among you, exercising oversight not under compulsion, but voluntarily, according to the will of God; and not for sordid gain, but with eagerness; nor yet as lording it over those allotted to your charge, but proving to be examples to the flock. And when the Chief Shepherd appears, you will receive the unfading crown of glory. You younger men, likewise, be subject to your elders; and all of you, clothe yourselves with humility toward one another, for GOD IS OPPOSED TO THE PROUD, BUT GIVES GRACE TO THE HUMBLE. (1 Peter 5:1–5)

---

[44] Even though there are elements in each passage that support each of these, for space purposes only one passage apiece will be considered for support of each characteristics in the life and ministry of one who is called to be a leader.

The passage is full of relational language and imagery that evokes the idea of care for others. However, notice three specific instances in which the importance of relating to people as a prerequisite for a ministry leadership is emphasized. First, Peter commanded elders to shepherd the flock that God had placed among them. Whatever your particular understanding of shepherding, and thus your philosophy of pastoral ministry, is, one would be hard-pressed to deny the obvious emphasis that the pastor must both know and care for the people he leads. As a matter of fact, the preposition used in this passage (*en*), may be better translated "with" and used to indicate association often related to "close personal relationship."[45] Furthermore, if they are with the pastor, then by definition the pastor must be with them.

Second, notice Peter seems to have concerned himself with not only what the pastor does but also with the motivation with which he does it. Peter communicated this by the use of three consecutive statements explaining how the pastor should shepherd contrasted with how he should not shepherd (see vv. 2–3). His discussion culminated with the statement, "Nor yet as lording it over those allotted to your charge, but proving to be examples to the flock." How do you set an example to the flock? Can an elder do so without being with the flock or without the flock being with him? Once more, the setting is relational. Peter was safeguarding against leadership abuse of the church.

Finally, Peter concluded the exhortation with the command "clothe yourselves with humility toward one another." Verse 5 may refer to all believers ("younger men") in the church and not to pastors only. However, we should understand that when something is required of all men, certainly no less it is expected of leaders. Therefore, what is the humility to which Peter referred and why does it matter for leaders? Perhaps the

---

[45] Wallace, *Greek Grammar Beyond the Basics*, 372.

best picture is found in Philippians 2. The example is Christ. "Have this attitude in yourselves which was also in Christ Jesus. . . . Being found in appearance as a man, He humbled Himself" (vv. 5, 8). The term used in this passage is related to that which is found in 1 Peter 5:5. Jesus "humiliated" himself. Why does this example matter for believers? The answer is given in Philippians 2:3: "Do nothing from selfishness or empty conceit, but with humility of mind regard one another as more important than yourselves." Pastors are to be those who show this kind of deference toward, and thus are an example to, others. Again, the axiom cannot be understood or practiced outside of the context of relationships. Not only was Jesus genuinely relatable, but ministry leaders must own this necessary characteristic as well.

A Leader Must Be Noticeably Honorable

With this in mind, what 1 Timothy 3:1–7 describes is noteworthy:

> It is a trustworthy statement: if any man aspires to the office of overseer, it is a fine work he desires to do. An overseer, then, must be above reproach, the husband of one wife, temperate, prudent, respectable, hospitable, able to teach, not addicted to wine or pugnacious, but gentle, peaceable, free from the love of money. He must be one who manages his own household well, keeping his children under control with all dignity (but if a man does not know how to manage his own household, how will he take care of the church of God?), and not a new convert, so that he will not become conceited and fall into the condemnation incurred by the devil. And he must have a good reputation with those outside the church, so that he will not fall into reproach and the snare of the devil.

With perhaps two exceptions,[46] everything else in the passages seems to be more about what type of person the overseer must be rather than the skills he must possess. The first characteristic mentioned in the list, then, is noteworthy. *Above reproach* (*anepilēmptos*) means "irreproachable" in relationship to conduct.[47] In common usage, the term can mean and is often translated "blameless" or even "unchargeable." "'Irreproachable' is general: 'not to be taken hold of,' i.e. of such a character that no one can rightfully take hold of the person with a charge of unfitness."[48] That it is first in the list may not be insignificant. In many ways, this concept appears to constitute all of and leads to the other qualifications. "To be 'above reproach' demanded that the overseer be a man of blameless character. . . . It may serve as a general, covering term for the following list of virtues that should distinguish a church leader."[49] Even if not formally, linguistically, or contextually so, functionally the term seems to be a summarization of the remainder of the passage covering the "character" qualifications of the pastor.[50] It seems clear that not only was Jesus noticeably honorable, but ministry leaders should strive for this characteristic as well.

---

[46] See "able to teach" in verse 2 and "one who manages his own household well" in verse 4.

[47] BDAG, 77.

[48] R. C. H. Lenski, *The Interpretation of St. Paul's Epistles to the Colossians, to the Thessalonians, to Timothy, to Titus, and to Philemon* (Minneapolis: Augsburg, 1964), 579.

[49] Thomas D. Lea and Hayne P. Griffin, Jr., *1, 2 Timothy, Titus*, The New American Commentary, vol. 34 (Nashville: B&H Publishing, 1992), 109.

[50] A more detailed version of this information appears in "Being Heard: How interpersonal relationship skills outside of the pulpit enhance your preaching in the pulpit," a contribution I wrote for a forthcoming update to Jeanine Cannon Bozeman and Argile Smith, eds. *Interpersonal Relationship Skills for Ministers* (Gretna, LA: Pelican Publishing Company, 2004). At the time of this writing, no publication date had been set for the book.

A Leader Must Be Competently Able

Reflecting back on the passage we just considered, a couple of skills or ability requirements are listed in this pastoral description. Perhaps, depending on how the concept is understood and applied, being a competent leader and manager could be included from verses 4–5. Certainly the term *manage (proistēmi)* can mean "to exercise a position of leadership, *rule, direct, be at the head (of)*."[51] That the author intended this meaning as a part of his point in these two verses seems obvious. However, that a relational aspect of leadership may be a part of the emphasis is possible as well. The usage and definition of the term allows for this option.[52] At least one scholar believes a focus on the character of the leader must be included in the understanding here. "For the father to see 'that his children obey him' does not demand excessive force or sternness. It demands primarily a character and manner of discipline that develop a natural respect."[53] Regardless of which interpretation is chosen for verse 4, one clear requirement is that the overseer possess the ability to understand and rightly teach the Word (1 Timothy 3:2). Even in a cursory reading of the list from 1 Timothy 3, then, one could argue that not only is "character" required but so is some manner of "skill."

With this in mind, consider the parallel list of qualifications in Titus 1:5–9:

> For this reason I left you in Crete, that you would set
> in order what remains and appoint elders in every city

---

[51] BDAG, 870.

[52] BDAG.

[53] Lea and Griffin, *1, 2 Timothy, Titus*, 112. A version of this information appears in my upcoming chapter "Being Heard," written for a forthcoming update to Bozeman and Smith, *Interpersonal Relationship Skills for Ministers*.

as I directed you, namely, if any man is above reproach, the husband of one wife, having children who believe, not accused of dissipation or rebellion. For the overseer must be above reproach as God's steward . . . holding fast the faithful word which is in accordance with the teaching, so that he will be able both to exhort in sound doctrine and to refute those who contradict.

This text is clear. The leader must possess competency in order to handle the challenges of ministry that he will face.[54] The qualification matches both the context and content of what we observed in 1 Timothy 3. Furthermore, the difficulty of the situation that Titus and those ministering on Crete faced was bleak. "For there are many rebellious men, empty talkers and deceivers, especially those of the circumcision, who must be silenced because they are upsetting whole families, teaching things they should not teach for the sake of sordid gain" (vv. 10–11). If this situation were not a dire one, it certainly would have been considered less than desirable and one in which a high level of skill would have been essential.

Not only was Jesus competently able, but ministry leaders must possess this characteristic too in order to lead successfully. Now that we have seen in both the ministry of Jesus and the requirements of elders that there are three necessary characteristics in order to develop the person of

---

[54] The point I am attempting to make from 1 Timothy 3 and Titus 1 is not that every leader, including women, must possess and practice the ability to teach the entire church. Rather, the conclusion is more general. Since God's Word specifically commands pastors to both display personal holiness and possess practical skills, the logic then follows that any ministry leader needs both character and ability. "Apt to teach" and "exhorting" and "correcting" doctrine, are intended as one representative example. One place, however, that the importance of having the skill of rightly handling the Word of God may be implied for women, and thus allows for a broader application to every ministry leader, is in the context of instructing or discipling other women in the church (See Titus 2:3–5).

ministry leadership, this chapter will conclude with some practical advice for developing these traits.

A Few Thoughts for Developing the Person of Leadership

It is imperative to realize that people are the focus in ministry leadership. A focus on getting things done or prioritizing tasks is not wrong or sinful in and of itself. As a matter of fact, sometimes in order to accomplish the mission of our ministry, tasks must be the focus. Furthermore, we need those among us who have a predisposition and skill set toward seeing and accomplishing the logistical and administrative components of the ministry. Approaches to being successful in these areas will be highlighted in other chapters in this book. However, a quality that often makes someone a great leader can also be a deterrent from the same person recognizing the goal of his or her leadership. The quality in question is being driven toward efficacy and productivity. Therefore, a leader must make a concerted effort to remember that all the tasks he or she takes up and all the productivity he or she measures is not the ultimate goal of ministry. Rather these things are for the sake of and to the service of the ultimate goal. So yes, be productive. Have processes and procedures. Guard your time and schedule meetings. However, remember the person who stops by the church every Tuesday after lunch is not a hindrance to the ministry. He is the ministry.

It is also important to make an intentional effort to be around the people you lead. If people are the focus of ministry, then being around them must be a priority. A leader needs to learn to do life with the people he leads. He must be a part of their lives and experiences, good and bad, and he needs to invite them into his life and experiences. This does not mean a leader should never have any time alone, should not prioritize his or her own family, or that he or she should exhaust people with his or her presence. However, this does mean the only time a leader's people see her must not be at church or during regularly scheduled ministry activities. Being around people is a necessary reminder of why we serve and who we lead. Furthermore, our presence is the only avenue through which we set genuine examples.

You must also work to recognize and minimize your leadership blind spots. Blind spots are weaknesses in our lives, personalities, and abilities we do not know exist. The good news is everyone has blind spots. The bad news is leaders are not immune to them, and blind spots usually are what derails a leader's ability to succeed. Often others can see a leader's blind spots, but he cannot diagnose himself. My desire as a leader has always been to have a perception of my leadership that grows toward other people's perception and, more importantly, reality. I want the gap between how I see myself and how others see me to be constantly shrinking, because that means my blind spots are shrinking. The first step toward strengthening and minimizing your weaknesses is to recognize them. For this reason, be willing to listen to other people's criticisms of you. One of my mentors, David Allen, has on occasion said, "When people criticize you they often miss the bullseye, but they hit the target." I have found this to be true. Even though at times doing so is difficult, be willing to listen to others. You will be glad you did, and you will grow from this practice.

This means you must commit to being a lifelong learner. This suggestion relates to the one in the previous paragraph because a commitment to continued growth and learning is the second part of the process in strengthening and minimizing weaknesses. Once you have discovered a blind spot, as foundational as this step is, you are only halfway through the process. You now need the tools, instructions, and abilities to correct the discovered weakness and to continue developing. For this and a number of other reasons, no one should desire to be a leader nor take up the task of leading who is not committed to being a lifelong learner. How this process occurs has some flexibility, but that it occurs is a necessity. While formal education and academic training is invaluable, attending conferences, joining training sessions, and reading regularly can also aid the process. But perhaps nothing can take the place of a relationship with a seasoned leader who has more experience than you do related to your area of ministry.

That's right. In order to develop as a leader, you must cultivate a relationship with a personal ministry mentor. This practice is not new. Paul believed in and argued for it in the life of Timothy. "The things which you have heard from me in the presence of many witnesses, entrust these to faithful men who will be able to teach others also" (2 Timothy 2:2). New Orleans Baptist Theological Seminary believes in mentoring and has an academic program built on this concept. However, mentoring adds value beyond the classroom. Actually, NOBTS believes in mentoring in the classroom primarily because of its benefits outside the classroom. A good mentor can help remind a leader that people are the focus of his ministry. A good mentor can point out when a leader fails to prioritize those she leads as well as some of her other blind spots. And a good mentor, in a practical real-life ministry leadership setting, can help a leader's commitment to lifelong learning through his own experiences. Your mentor can be the single most helpful ingredient in your ministry for helping you develop the person of leadership and grow in your relatability, honorability, and overall ability.

Case Study

After spending a significant amount of time developing and writing your philosophy of leadership that will guide your path and a specific process for biblical leadership issues, you now have begun recasting a new ten-year ministry plan for Third Baptist Church of Somewhere, America. As you begin to discuss the mission, vision, goals, and measurements of success with the leadership team and other individuals in the congregation, you run into opposition you never imagined or anticipated. The opposition can be categorized by three distinct groups, but each relates to the person of leadership.

Because of the recent challenges you faced related to family, community, ministry stresses, and life in general that led to a bit of a "calling crisis," you took some time away from ministry. As a result, the first group questions whether or not you have spent enough time reengaging the congregation personally. They are not completely against the new mission and ministry focus, but they believe your first priority should be ministering to the flock. They believe before you can know what the church needs you must reacquaint yourself with them and let them learn to follow you again.

The second group questions whether or not you were completely honest and accurate about the stresses you said you experienced in the first place. They wonder if these things should have taken you away from your responsibilities or if you blew them out of proportion a little bit. After all, they cannot simply take free time off work just because they feel "blue."

The final group does not have a problem with the new ministry focus. As a matter of fact, they completely agree with the plans and believe it is past time to get to work. Their problem is not even that they do not like you personally. They do, however, wonder whether you have the skills necessary to plan and carry out such an undertaking for the entire church, especially considering your recent experiences.

Using the information from this chapter, write a response for how you would build or display the person of leadership in response to each group's concern. Be specific, and be sure to include support as to why you will choose this path. You may supplement your answer with other information and sources, but be sure to include information from our study in chapter 4, especially as it relates to the three necessary characteristics of biblical leadership.

Chapter 5

Ministering to the People

During high school, my mentor asked me to complete a personal reflection exercise introduced by Stephen Covey. I was to consider my funeral and the different people in the room—family, friends, colleagues, and acquaintances. It was surreal to think about my funeral and what people would remember about me. The different ways I lived among these friends have forever been in my mind as I reflect on the importance of character development. Leadership expert Carey Nieuwhof references this same exercise and concludes, "The crowd is intrigued by your competency, but your family and close friends are influenced by your character."[55] The ways we minister to people creates a legacy of character that will outlive our best teaching or sermons.

Each week, unexpected events happen in ministry: a funeral, a tragic accident, and even facility problems. These events certainly require our attention, but if we do not figure out a plan to prioritize the most critical items, the unexpected may cause pressure and fatigue. In this chapter, we will explore how to develop your weekly schedule or workflow to accomplish your goals while also being available to minister to your people.

---

[55] Carey Nieuwhof, *Didn't See It Coming: Overcoming the 7 Greatest Challenges That No One Expects and Everyone Experiences* (New York: Waterbrook, 2018), 39.

Ministers are often required to function much like an emergency room physician, tasked with evaluating and triaging patients based on the level of care needed. Physicians must determine who to treat first—a child with a potential broken arm, an elderly gentleman suffering a heart attack, or a victim of an unfortunate car accident with numerous injuries. Ministers face similar circumstances during an average week: a toilet overflowing in the preschool area, an unexpected death of a church member, and a church family whose teenager was involved in a car accident. Each of these instances will take time from your week as you navigate your time and responsibilities to keep the main focus on target. How do we prioritize ministry circumstances while keeping people as the essential aspect of our work?

Some years ago, Charles Tidwell wrote practical words that are still true today as we consider the ministry's administrative aspects:

> A Church is of God and people. Church administration concerns itself with presenting the human element in the partnership equation as a disciplined, orderly, purposeful instrument to be directed and used of God as He sees fit. Church administration concerns itself with the overall guidance provided by church leaders as they utilize the spiritual, human, physical, and financial resources of the church to move toward fulfilling its purpose and objectives. On the human plane, church resources are limited. The limitation of resources makes the management of them more imperative.[56]

The Bible provides numerous examples of managing ministry responsibilities between people and projects, essential and urgent. Mary and Martha provide differing perspectives of

---

[56] Charles Tidwell, *Church Administration: Effective Leadership for Ministry* (Nashville: Broadman Press, 1985), 12.

doing the work and being with the people, which included spending time with Jesus. Among the chosen twelve disciples, we see the struggle of ministry through feeding people and ministering to the physical needs through a meal for thousands. In the early church, Christians sold resources and shared all they had so no one had a need to remain unmet. The theological backdrop of these examples varies, but the reality for each of us as ministry leaders is a practical consideration. When the unexpected happens, will we be people who run to sit at the feet of Jesus or one who busies ourselves to complete a project? Will you be a person who deliberates the cost of ministry to others or serves others in faith of God's provision? Are your own needs given priority or the needs of those around you? Let's unpack some of these topics to better understand our role as leaders in ministry: managing the unexpected, ministering through crisis, managing the overall ministry components, and ministering to the people who make it all happen each week.

Managing the Unexpected

Unexpected circumstances can quickly cause us to become ministers of fear rather than ministry leaders. Weather, health crises, people issues, facility problems, financial concerns, and factors beyond our comprehension can challenge our ministry leadership. In our current ministry climate, a healthy understanding of common sense is needed to manage the unexpected. Society questions leadership credibility through billboard lawyers who suggest leaders and organizations cannot protect those under their care. Although we hear about churches and ministries sued for negligence, abuse, and fraud, unexpected circumstances cast a broader net of potential problems in our ministry administration. Each week we must consider our worship services, program-based ministries, discipleship structures, and upcoming events. Similarly, a tornado does not discriminate its path of destruction. Unexpected circumstances do not discriminate in our ministries. It does not matter how many people attend our church, the size of our facilities, or our fiscal structures' effectiveness. We must possess the flexibility to manage whatever unexpected circumstance comes our way.

The church should always plan to deal with any weather emergency—a fire escape plan, tornado evacuation plan, and even plans for an active shooter situation. Additionally, churches should be prepared to handle a health crisis. Crises can be a simple one-person instance of someone falling in the hallway, a child breaking an arm on the playground, or something more complicated, such as a heart attack during worship. Health emergencies can also happen during church events such as a mission trip or summer camp. Over the years, different countries have had health-related concerns that caused people to have preventative care and shots before a mission trip to prepare for unexpected health emergencies while traveling. In recent years, we have been reminded that health-related problems can be widespread and cause large-scale concerns with seemingly normal activities such as gathering together for worship. How would your church continue to gather if physical gatherings were not possible due to health concerns? Take a few moments to consider possible unexpected events in your ministry, and then take some time to pray for your congregation and personal leadership responsibilities.

Ministering through a Crisis

What constitutes a crisis? Crises run a broad mixture of needs, situations, and severities. Any given day in the church office, a person needing benevolence is walking through a personal crisis, looking to the church for assistance. In a congregation, everyone struggles when a leader has a moral failure, forcing the church into crisis mode. In a community, crises occur when a weather disaster strikes and people lose their homes or lives. The whole region is walking through a crisis. An economic downturn may force a nation into crisis, while a global pandemic can cause widespread concerns worldwide. Many turn to news media to better understand the situation and determine how a global crisis may affect them personally.

Weather emergencies present a unique situation where you have little time to prepare, and people are quickly propelled into crisis mode. Often, people from all over the nation or world rush to minister and provide resources to the affected people's physical, emotional, and spiritual needs in a crisis. Pandemics remind us of the plagues that have impacted humanity for thousands of years and each century of modern history. Health-related pandemics are more difficult for us to navigate, as we have to weigh shepherding our people, practice personal care, and maintain a compassionate desire to meet together and do the work of ministry.

Ministers provide strength, hope, peace, and calm amid a crisis. In the church, leaders need to remember to minister to each aspect of a crisis, whether it involves one family, a few families, the community, a nation, or the world. Each situation can provide incredible ministry opportunities depending on our preparation level—administrative preparation through both fiscal resources and the chain of command is essential to lead through a crisis. The initial impact of a crisis is only one aspect of our ministry to people. Whether at the hospital with a family navigating the death of a loved one or in a city ravaged by a tornado, people are generally more open to personal assistance as they navigate their situation or circumstances. Also, people are usually more open to spiritual counsel and support during times of difficulty.

Managing the Overall Ministry Components

Oversight is essential to accomplish ministry goals. Issues or concerns may arise if proper attention is not given to leadership and management. As with each area of administration, keeping a balance between people and tasks cannot be understated. Volunteer or paid personnel need to be trained and coached in how to lead their ministry area. A ministry audit is a helpful tool to evaluate the health, direction, and success of each ministry element or focus area in your church. Leaders should ensure each ministry element fits with the overall approach of your church's corporate strategy for the congregation. Fiscal and physical resources should also be considered when managing the big picture. Leadership and management have to be well-connected when managing the overall direction and structure of the church.

Ministry teams are often asked to manage church resources. Each organization has facilities, finances, and people that have to be managed. Allocating these resources for each ministry can be a challenge. Many people do not like the details required to manage the resources of the organization. Money, volunteers, and facilities can be challenging and take a lot of a leader's time. Some ministers are not administratively gifted and struggle with managing finances, training volunteers, and evaluating the facilities for ministry schedules. Thankfully, the facilities and the finances usually have dedicated people to account for the cleaning and maintaining of the property. A financial team often provides oversight for the counting of tithes and offerings, with a dedicated process for receiving and distributing the church's budgeted funds. The managing of volunteers and paid staff in the church is the largest component of any given week. When you calculate all the donated hours each week by volunteers in the church, the most significant resource is always the people. The challenge is how to manage a volunteer workforce that is busy with many moving parts in their lives and schedules each week.

Ministering to the People that Make It Happen Each Week

People are a priority. Each week, the human resource component of ministry cannot be left to chance. The volunteers and staff need to be trained and coached. We can connect to our volunteer leaders and team members through virtual resources that can be pushed to them individually. Video-driven training, video conference meetings, and digital resources provide a wealth of information and support the in-person training and coaching of ministry staff. Resources like these help staff and volunteers stay connected as we serve together but should never replace in-person relationship building. We must be good stewards of how we leverage technology for engaging and equipping our people each week. Necessity moves us toward technology, but we have to be wise in using a group text or app as a connecting point versus more personal ways. Each generation has their preferences in how they desire to connect.

If we can manage the unexpected, minister through the crisis, manage all the moving parts, and minister to the people, then we should be able to minister to all the people in a systematic way that models Acts 6 by not having a group of people whose needs have been left out or forgotten. We should rise above the unexpected and not be derailed by something tragic but instead move forward with steady leadership that shepherds the people along. The reality is each one of these four areas can be consuming and cause another area of ministry to suffer. The challenge is learning to entrust others and develop ministry leaders to navigate the various challenges the church, congregation, and leaders will face.

The following challenge found in the book *Didn't See It Coming* describes this best:

> People will remember if you loved well, if you forgave easily, if you cared enough to be there for them. They'll remember if you served or preferred to be served. They'll know whether you thought life revolved around you or whether you really tried to honor God and others. They'll remember whether you were generous or miserly, arrogant or humble, compassionate or indifferent. They'll remember your temper or whether you learned the rhythms of grace.[57]

Ministry through Coaching

Coaching is a unique dynamic in the world today. From an early age, children can participate in various team sports where a coach will lead them. Sometimes these coaches are parents who volunteer their time to help their child's team. Other times, coaches are employed by local parks and recreation departments, schools, or community organizations. Another component of children's athletics involves travel teams, where families pay the coaches. Teenagers can be involved in school athletics, and there are numerous ways teenagers can be associated with a coach who invests in their lives through the lens of sports. As athletes mature and advance into college or professional leagues, coaches are still an essential part of the experience. Both college and professional athletics have coaches who provide leadership, strategy, and corrective guidance. Some organizations have trainers or individual mentors who work to develop athletes' skills. I love watching

---

[57] Nieuwhof, *Didn't See It Coming*, 40.

college football, basketball, and baseball. Some coaches are comical to watch, others are disciplined, and others act as though they need anger management counseling. I remember the joy of watching Steve Spurrier get enraged and then take and slam his visor during Florida football games. Nick Saban is the "angry headset throwing coach" who is comical to watch. These men get enraged over their players, teams, and referees to the extent that, as a coach, they cannot control their emotions.

A coach is to be the key person to develop individual athletes, so the whole team thrives. Do you believe the heart of coaching should be to win or to develop talent? Monday-morning quarterbacks always talk about the scorecard and what could have been executed differently by a coach that lost. Many times, as fans, we get focused on the meaning of coaching as the intended winning outcome for our team. In the church, the goal should be coaching to develop the talents and gifts within our sphere of influence. As leaders and volunteers, we should be willing to be coached to grow as a leader and serve the body of Christ. We should also remember that people around us observe our actions to see our behaviors toward circumstances that can enhance or discredit our ability to coach others.

A small group leader, volunteer, chaperone, or dedicated intern can function as a coach who develops other leaders to use their gifts and talents. Ministry is dependent upon people in each of these roles. The church could not function and have ministries without people who volunteer to use their gifts to advance God's kingdom. People using their skills to serve is how Paul described the church functioning to achieve God's overall mission. In Ephesians 4, Paul described the various gifts and discerned that each Christian should be serving in the church by using their unique, spiritual gifting for kingdom purposes. Different gifts are also described with instructions for achieving church unity through everyone serving and giving everything they have. As a coach in ministry, we should help others discover and develop their spiritual gifts.

Reflect on these words from Ephesians:

> Therefore each of you must put off falsehood and speak truthfully to your neighbor, for we are all members of one body. "In your anger do not sin": Do not let the sun go down while you are still angry, and do not give the devil a foothold. Anyone who has been stealing must steal no longer, but must work, doing something useful with their own hands, that they may have something to share with those in need. Do not let any unwholesome talk come out of your mouths, but only what is helpful for building others up according to their needs, that it may benefit those who listen. And do not grieve the Holy Spirit of God, with whom you were sealed for the day of redemption. Get rid of all bitterness, rage and anger, brawling and slander, along with every form of malice. Be kind and compassionate to one another, forgiving each other, just as in Christ God forgave you. Follow God's example, therefore, as dearly loved children and walk in the way of love, just as Christ loved us and gave himself up for us a fragrant offering and sacrifice to God. But among you there must not be even a hint of sexual immorality, or of any kind of impurity, or of greed, because these are improper for God's holy people. Nor should there be obscenity, foolish talk or coarse joking, which are out of place, but rather thanksgiving. (4:25–5:4 NIV)

Our mission as ministry leaders and volunteers is similar to that of adult ministry: how to be unified in the church, love our neighbor, and grow in maturity as a disciple of Christ for his worldwide mission. Minors are often considered the church's future and not coached to serve as the church of today. We should be a role model who reflects our relationship with Christ and who walks in the light. Just like athletes will mess up in a competition or coaches may have a bad moment, we should coach our ministry teams through difficulty. A coach for leaders in the church has to be a person who reflects Christ in every area of life. We cannot have hints of anything from a sinful life that would discredit the work God has called us to or break the unity in the body of Christ. Disciple leaders in the church must be able to watch and emulate their ministry coaches.

Coaches bear strengths and weaknesses in the same way we do as ministry leaders. We all find ourselves in need of mentoring, encouragement, instruction, and discipline. Some coaches do all four of these well or excel in one of the four aspects. I remember a basketball coach who had passion and drive but was limited in personal encouragement, mentoring, and discipline. The result was a short-sighted perspective on our team and the goals we were trying to achieve. A ministry volunteer or employee expects the people they work with will provide the needed direction to thrive in the role they are serving. A coach who values the people on the team will provide these needs for their team. The people of the church also expect that those serving in ministry will mentor, encourage, instruct, and provide corrective counsel when their life is struggling. Coaching in ministry requires ongoing learning and development and the flexibility to coach in different ways.

Mentoring is one way to coach in ministry and is a term that can be interchanged with *coach* to develop people in Christ to mature in their faith and lead well using their unique God-given resources to serve. Developing ourselves and others should become a natural part of our ministry. Paul could name many people in his ministry who were lay leaders and a part of his ministry team. Timothy and Paul's relationship is one of my favorites in scripture. Paul is a seasoned leader who takes a younger inexperienced leader and invests richly into his life. This relationship has become an influential ministry relationship. Each ministry leader should have people they mentor, people who they naturally pour their life in Christ and ministry experience into as they live out their lives for Christ. In my life, there have been some older laymen or pastors who have naturally coached me to develop in relationships, skills, goals, and responsibilities to become a more committed follower of Christ. The unique aspect of my mentors is that most started pouring into me when I was a teenager. These mentors have continued to invest in my life today. If you can help people see the ministry narrative is more about developing people to become like Christ and not merely fill a space or event with people, the kingdom wins. If we can name the people more than we can count the numbers, the coaching metric is more like what Paul taught us through mentoring others.

Another way to coach others is to be an encourager. The style and format of encouragement has been debated as some coaches get heated or riled up at a player, another coach, or official during a game. The ability to lean in and coach or teach someone is a different type of encouragement from simply being emotional during a game. Encouragement in ministry is a necessary component of coaching. In the church, this style of communication is not the preferred coaching method. In our encounters, we should encourage one another toward Christlikeness and build one another up. Inspiring leaders and volunteers will enhance the people as well as leaders to be more like Christ. They will also become a person of influence because people desire to be around them.

Barnabas was known as an encourager (Acts 4:36). And Paul captured the essence of what should define us as ministry coaches:

> Therefore if you have any encouragement from being united with Christ, if any comfort from his love, if

any common sharing in the Spirit, if any tenderness and compassion, then make my joy complete by being like-minded, having the same love, being one in spirit and of one mind. Do nothing out of selfish ambition or vain conceit. Rather, in humility value others above yourselves, not looking to your own interests but each of you to the interests of the others. (Philippians 2:1–4 NIV)

Being a coach who encourages others requires selflessness and humility as we help others press on in their spiritual walk.

Instruction is a vital component of coaching. Without understanding the plays and strategy for both offense and defense, the game becomes haphazard and disorganized. A coach teaches the necessary skills of the sport and develops the talent of the players. As a ministry coach, both staff and volunteers need instruction. A ministry volunteer needs education about the expectations of their area of ministry. People need to be taught how to navigate God's Word and how to live life as a Christian. We receive instruction from many people, and we pray the primary place for Christian education is in the home. Each person has leaders beyond the church through extracurricular activities, athletics, hobbies, and organizations that also have influence. All of these voices from parents, friends, school, fitness tribes, hobby groups, and other activities are important, but the church instructors may be the only Christian instruction they receive.

Corrective coaching can be a challenge when dealing with a host of volunteers, personalities, and spiritual maturity levels. Discipline in ministry is one aspect of coaching that the church can struggle in navigating. Social media and the internet have created a wave of people sharing their opinions, habits, lifestyle, and much more than what we used to know about people unless it came up in conversation. The Bible shares accounts and instructions for providing correction or discipline when a person is a leader and does not live up to the standard for ministry conduct described in the Bible. In the letters to Timothy, overseers and deacons were described with specific lifestyle requirements.

Similarly, ministry leaders and volunteers should also strive to live a life worthy of respect and with all sincerity and should not indulge or pursue dishonest gain. They should also have beliefs that align with church theology that they exhibit in their Christian life. As we encounter ministry leaders or volunteers who have a questionable area of their life, we should strive to help them and restore them in their walk with Christ. Since disciples can be vulnerable in their spiritual maturity, we also need to help them if they are struggling or help shelter them from leaders who are in a season of personal struggle and do not meet the standard for an adult serving in ministry.

Questions for Reflection

1. Coaches develop, mentor, encourage, instruct, and correct. What type of coach are you?

2. As ministry leaders, do we desire to win at our perspectives for ministry or develop the people to be mature disciples who use their gifts for the kingdom through the local church?

3. How does your approach to the administrative work reveal a longing for your people to perceive your heart's desire to minister to them and their needs?

Chapter 6

Defining Biblical Standards for Leading People

Remember leadership is both who you are and what you do. A leader must display consistent and dependable patterns in her or his actions if he or she expects to be followed. Consider the following example. You may believe a certain individual is a person of the highest integrity, but knowing she does not have a pilot's license, you do not trust her to fly you home for the holidays. You would be wise and correct in your hesitation. To lead, then, a person must not just be trusted but must be trusted to accomplish certain tasks. We examined the person of leadership in chapter 4 and focused on the need to possess certain personal qualities in your leadership. In this chapter, we will examine the other side of the equation. That is, in leadership your actions must also display consistent trustworthy principles and kingdom-minded patterns. We will explore in detail the primary principles of leadership, namely the practice of leadership, which is foundational for effective ministry leadership.

That the practice of leadership (what a leader does) is needed in a leader's ability to influence followers and necessary for accomplishing tasks in biblical leadership is clear. Recalling chapter 2, Aubrey Malphurs, in his work

Being Leaders, wrote that a key component of leadership is credibility. He continued and argued that another key component of leadership is capability. "What makes one a super leader and another an average leader? I believe that a major factor is what a leader brings to a church or parachurch ministry—his or her capabilities."[58] His description of what capabilities are may be helpful for our understanding. "Capabilities include spiritual and natural gifts, passion, temperament, knowledge, skills, and emotions. They are important because they position the leader to do something eternally significant for God and his kingdom, to have kingdom impact."[59] Once more, difference certainly exists between Malphurs's approach and our perspective. However, his description is helpful. What a leader does, and whether or not he or she does so with an eternal perspective, is critical to leadership. Leadership tasks, and thus leadership holistically, is impacted not only by who a leader is but also by what a leader does and how he or she does it.

Do we see the practice of leadership in the ministry leadership of Jesus? Is there a "what he does" component in the ministry of Christ? I believe there is. In him, we can find at least three primary principles of leadership. In this chapter, our description of biblical leadership in light of what a leader does, the practice of leadership, will be considered. For this approach, the three primary principles of leadership will be identified first through an examination of Jesus's leadership. The principles are: he had God's goal instead of simply a good goal; he valued people over production; and he never sacrificed the eternal for the temporal. We begin by examining these principles in the life and ministry of Jesus.

---

[58] Aubrey Malphurs, *Being Leaders: The Nature of Authentic Christian Leadership* (Grand Rapids: Baker Books, 2003), 73.
[59] Malphurs, 74.

The Three Primary Principles of Leadership in the Example of Jesus

He Had God's Goal Instead of Simply a Good Goal

The tendency here may be to begin by asking the question, "What is God's goal?" What did God send Jesus to do? What is the Father's highest commitment? In context, not only is this an obvious question, but we may also feel as though it comparatively is easily answered. More than likely, a high percentage of those reading this book would arrive at the same general answer. However, for reasons I hope will become clear as these principles are defined, I do not want to begin with this question. Before looking at what the goal is, we will observe Jesus's unquestioning and unwavering obedience to the Father and thus his commitment to what the Father commanded. Perhaps no passage illustrates this more vividly than John 4:31–38:

> Meanwhile the disciples were urging Him, saying, "Rabbi, eat." But He said to them, "I have food to eat that you do not know about." So the disciples were saying to one another, "No one brought Him anything to eat, did he?" Jesus said to them, "My food is to do the will of Him who sent Me and to accomplish His work. Do you not say, 'There are yet four months, and then comes the harvest'? Behold, I say to you, lift up your eyes and look on the fields, that they are white for harvest. Already he who reaps is receiving wages and is gathering fruit for life eternal; so that he who sows and he who reaps may rejoice together. For in this case the saying is true, 'One sows and another reaps.' I sent you to reap that for which you have not labored; others have labored and you have entered into their labor."

On a basic level, this passage is not hard to understand. Jesus taught his disciples about his commitment and to what he is committed. The way he chose to do so is unique. He did so through the metaphor of food and the act of eating.

Remember the context. At the beginning of the chapter, Jesus had traveled through Samaria on his journey from Judea to Galilee to escape the jealousy of the Pharisees.[60] After stopping near the Samaritan city of Sychar, Jesus sent his disciples into the city to buy dinner. About this time, a Samaritan woman came to the well to draw water. This leads to a surprising gospel conversation between Jesus and the woman. At some point after the conversation, the disciples returned with the evening meal and urged Jesus to eat. Jesus used this meal as a teachable moment and engaged them in dialogue, which our passage records for us. Notice three takeaways from this passage: the confusion from the disciples about what Jesus was really talking about, the clarity of Jesus that the will and work of the Father are gospel-related, and the ultimate calling of Jesus to the disciples for them to join him in submitting to the will and work of the Father.

First, the disciples were amazed if not outright confused when Jesus said he had already eaten. They pleaded with their master, who was weary when they left, to take and be sustained by that which they had brought back. He refused and explained that he had food to eat that they knew nothing about. At this moment, they thought he was talking about physical food and wondered where this food could have come from. Jesus responded by explaining that the food to which he was referring is doing the will of the Father and accomplishing the work of the Father. Essentially Jesus was using a metaphor to explain following and obeying the Father is food, like eating, for him. This sustained him. It nourished him. This action was not novel in Jesus's ministry. Rather it was his consistent pattern. We see it in other places

---

[60] Because of their public disdain for Samaritans, this path would have been an unusual one for a Jew to take.

throughout his ministry. "I can do nothing on My own initiative. As I hear, I judge; and My judgment is just, because I do not seek My own will, but the will of Him who sent Me" (John 5:30). This commitment was also still on display for us at the end of this ministry, profoundly so in the garden on the night of his arrest. "And He went a little beyond them, and fell on His face and prayed, saying, 'My Father, if it is possible, let this cup pass from Me; yet not as I will, but as You will'" (Matthew 26:39).

Second, Jesus emphasized that the will and work of the Father are gospel-related. Interestingly yet not surprisingly, the passages that display Jesus's obedience to the Father's will and his commitment to his goal always seem related to the mission of God and that which relates to the redemption of men. In the John 4 passage, the dialogue between Jesus and his disciples took place on the heels of his conversation with a Samaritan woman. That interaction culminated with a clear gospel application. "The woman said to Him, 'I know that Messiah is coming (He who is called Christ); when that One comes, He will declare all things to us.' Jesus said to her, 'I who speak to you am He'" (John 4:25–26). Afterwards, in an apparent connection to this dialogue, Jesus said to his disciples that he had food from his Father when he was offered dinner by his disciples. Furthermore, what he next described as the will and work of him who sent him is a kind of harvest. This harvest is a metaphor not for crops or wheat, but for the souls of men.[61] That Jesus meant a soul harvest by this imagery is consistent with his direct reference to receiving wages and gathering fruit for eternal life.

Finally, Jesus called his disciples to join him in submitting to the will and work of the Father. The point Jesus made to

---

[61] See parallel passage in Matthew 9. In verses 35–38, the meaning of the harvest metaphor as "a harvest of men" or "a gospel harvest" seems clear and obvious.

the disciples seems not to be ultimately what sustains and nourishes him. Rather the application he made is what should sustain and nourish them. The question the disciples implied was, "What is your food?" Jesus, however, like in so many other places, ultimately did not answer the question they asked. He answered another one. He took them a step further than they intended to go. The question he answered was related to their question for sure but different nonetheless. Jesus showed them what their food should be. "Behold, I say to you, lift up your eyes and look on the fields, that they are white for harvest. . . . I sent you to reap that for which you have not labored; others have labored and you have entered into their labor" (vv. 35, 38).[62] The ultimate point Jesus made to the disciples was their obedience to the will of God and their commitment to the work of the Father, both of which he modeled for them. Jesus had God's goal instead of simply a good goal, and he called his followers to the same.

He Valued People Over Production

The second principle exemplified in Jesus's ministry leadership is that he valued people over production. If Jesus ever had a time in which he could have justified being task-oriented, then the events of Luke 19 are it. This was his death march, his final journey to Jerusalem, if you will. He was going to die in obedience to his Father and fulfill his greatest mission to date. By the end of the chapter, he will have experienced the Triumphal Entry, which we now know only preceded his lonely crucifixion. Therefore, in this setting we may even say that not only would it be acceptable for Jesus to have a laser-like focus, but we should expect nothing less.

---

[62] Once again, see Matthew 9:35–38 where Jesus's call for his disciples to be workers in the harvest seems even more clear and explicit.

Perhaps, then, in the context of Jesus's paschal trip to the Holy City, we move beyond permission to expectation. We demand, here if anywhere, that the Messiah be task-oriented. We expect ultimate productivity. He should have been single-minded. We want him to avoid any and all distractions. Nevertheless, instead we read of an unexpected detour.

> He entered Jericho and was passing through. And there was a man called by the name of Zaccheus; he was a chief tax collector and he was rich. Zaccheus was trying to see who Jesus was, and was unable because of the crowd, for he was small in stature. So he ran on ahead and climbed up into a sycamore tree in order to see Him, for He was about to pass through that way. When Jesus came to the place, He looked up and said to him, "Zaccheus, hurry and come down, for today I must stay at your house." And he hurried and came down and received Him gladly. When they saw it, they all began to grumble, saying, "He has gone to be the guest of a man who is a sinner." Zaccheus stopped and said to the Lord, "Behold, Lord, half of my possessions I will give to the poor, and if I have defrauded anyone of anything, I will give back four times as much." And Jesus said to him, "Today salvation has come to this house, because he, too, is a son of Abraham. For the Son of Man has come to seek and to save that which was lost." (Luke 19:1–10)

On the road to Golgotha, Jesus stopped. He took time to notice, converse with, and even fellowship with Zaccheus. Why would Jesus turn aside? How could Jesus abandon his people and certainly delay his progress on the path to his mission, his ultimate productivity, for this one man? The reason why is because Zaccheus was the aim or reason for his task. He was on a journey, a mission, to die for the redemption of Zaccheus and others like him. The purchase of this man's soul and the eternal redemption of men was his task and his greatest concern in the moment. Furthermore, in case you think the care for individuals, even those who are considered the least valuable and most vulnerable in society, was rare or unusual for our Savior, consider this passage: "Then some children were brought to Him so that He might lay His hands on them and pray; and the disciples rebuked them. But Jesus said, 'Let the children alone, and do not hinder them from coming to Me; for the kingdom of heaven belongs to such as these.' After laying His hands on them, He departed from there" (Matthew 19:13–14). People were the product for Jesus and the recognition and meeting of their greatest need was the productivity he prioritized. Jesus valued people over production, and he set the example for us as ministry leaders to do the same.

He Never Sacrificed the Eternal for the Temporal

Based on his interaction with Zaccheus, and even his teaching regarding the children, a natural interpretation would be that Jesus always gave people what they sought. He never abandoned or walked away from a need, and certainly not a legitimate one. Jesus touched people where they felt the greatest want. He always met all the physical needs of people. He took care of what people perceived they lacked the most and thus would bring the most significance to their lives. In the Gospels, Jesus constantly and consistently met everyone's physical needs; therefore, he certainly will meet every need that you, I, and everyone else have today. However, we know this is simply not the case. Not surprisingly, we know this is not true experientially. Perhaps surprisingly, it is not true biblically either. If you think otherwise, there are at least two passages to consider. In the first, Jesus departed from those who were seeking healing from him. In the second, those who came to Jesus departed from him without receiving what they sought.

First, consider Mark 1:32–39. The background is important. After his baptism, Jesus began his public ministry. Perhaps the best summary of this ministry, including its aim, is recorded in verses 14 and 15 of the same chapter: "Now after John had been taken into custody, Jesus came into Galilee, preaching the gospel of God, and saying, 'The time is fulfilled, and the kingdom of God is at hand; repent and believe the gospel.'" Leading to the cross, his ministry was one of proclamation, calling sinners to repent of sin and preparing people to receive eternal life through his sacrifice and atonement. His acts also included calling disciples, teaching in synagogues, and casting out demons. Eventually, he moved to Capernaum, Peter's hometown. Not only did Capernaum become the headquarters of Jesus's ministry, the location also became the place where for a time most of his teaching and work was concentrated. The popularity this gained for Jesus led, apparently quickly, to large crowds recognizing him and seeking him for physical healings and relief from the demonic. "When evening came, after the sun had set, they began bringing to Him all who were ill and those who were demon-possessed. And the whole city had gathered at the door. And He healed many who were ill with various diseases, and cast out many demons; and He was not permitting the demons to speak, because they knew who He was" (vv. 32–34).

Factoring in what we think we know about Jesus, what would we expect to be his next move? To set up shop, right? Perhaps we would expect him to enjoy the opportunity this afforded and to continue this benevolence ministry. Listen to what happened next.

> In the early morning, while it was still dark, Jesus got up, left the house, and went away to a secluded place, and was praying there. Simon and his companions searched for Him; they found Him, and said to Him, "Everyone is

looking for You." He said to them, "*Let us go somewhere else to the towns nearby, so that I may preach there also; for that is what I came for.*" And He went into their synagogues throughout all Galilee, preaching and casting out the demons. (vv. 35–39, emphasis added)

To be fair, two caveats to our approach to the passage must be acknowledged. One is that Jesus's real concern could not have been a problem with healing people or meeting their physical needs alone. Actually, he continued to heal people and cast out demons. The text says in verse 39 that casting out demons continued to be a regular part of his ministry in other locations. Furthermore, the next section of scripture describes a specific healing of a leprous man.[63] Jesus did not lose his compassion for people or concern for their physical well-being. The problem was the distraction to his ultimate mission that the popularity associated with such actions in Capernaum had created. Nonetheless, as we will see in a moment, this fact does not change the overall emphasis, which is seen in Jesus's mission. The second caveat is that Jesus's statement of purpose in verse 38 is consistent with and parallel to his mission focus at large to this point in his public ministry. Again, the issue was not a lack of care for people and their poor physical state. The issue was his concern for something more significant. He cared about them at a deeper level than they could understand. He knew they had a greater need that no one else could address. He stayed focused on solving a problem in which both the need and the solution extends past the immediate.

In case you are tempted to believe this is an isolated event or that I am being unfair by "proof-texting" here, consider also John 6. The chapter begins with Jesus meeting a physical and immediate need in a miraculous way. Jesus fed five

---

[63] See Mark 1:40–45.

thousand with five loaves and two fish (vv. 1–14). Then on the next day, the same crowd came again to Jesus on the other side of the sea, where Jesus had arrived overnight by way of a second miracle. At the beginning of the second encounter, the crowds recognized and acknowledged this miracle as well: "When they found Him on the other side of the sea, they said to Him, 'Rabbi, when did You get here?'" (v. 25). The problem that we now know is that they came not because they were seeking Jesus but because they wanted a repeat of the previous day's benefits. Jesus immediately recognized their motives. "Jesus answered them and said, 'Truly, truly, I say to you, you seek Me, not because you saw signs, but because you ate of the loaves and were filled'" (v. 26).

Perhaps in a somewhat surprising move, he refused their request, but not before turning this interaction into a teachable moment. "Do not work for the food which perishes, but for the food which endures to eternal life, which the Son of Man will give to you, for on Him the Father, God, has set His seal" (v. 27). He used their physical quest for food to point them to their spiritual need and the possibility of having that need met in him (vv. 35–40). Ultimately, he told the crowds following him that he was all they would get, but he was all they needed.

> Truly, truly, I say to you, unless you eat the flesh of the Son of Man and drink His blood, you have no life in yourselves. He who eats My flesh and drinks My blood has eternal life, and I will raise him up on the last day. For My flesh is true food, and My blood is true drink. He who eats My flesh and drinks My blood abides in Me, and I in him. As the living Father sent Me, and I live because of the Father, so he who eats Me, he also will live because of Me. This is the bread which came down out of heaven; not as the fathers ate and died; he who eats this bread will live forever. (vv. 53–58)

What was the result? What was the response to this shocking and borderline absurd revelation of even many of those who were following him at this time? They went away. They left and no longer followed him (v. 66). The final interaction between Jesus and the twelve, represented here in the person of Peter, is noteworthy and helpful for us: "So Jesus said to the twelve, 'You do not want to go away also, do you?' Simon Peter answered Him, 'Lord, to whom shall we go? *You have words of eternal life.* We have believed and have come to know that You are the Holy One of God'" (vv. 67–69, emphasis added). Once again, the issue was not Jesus's lack of care for people's basic and physical needs. Jesus was focused on something else. This other focus was communicated and emphasized through the words of Peter when he spoke for the group. The issue was that Jesus was not motivated by temporal needs and thus ones that could only be addressed temporally. For the sake of the greater, Jesus never sacrificed the eternal for the temporal.

Perhaps we do not want to assign motives. We do not want to assume more than these texts allow. Of all else that may be deduced, at a minimum two conclusions must be acknowledged. First, although Jesus cared for people deeply and often ministered to them on a physical level, he did not always turn aside to meet every request, even legitimate and immediate needs. Second, Jesus refused to be distracted from what he knew to be his ultimate mission. He would not be drawn away from God's goal for him. He never sacrificed the eternal for the temporal. The question that remains is, How do we reconcile these conclusions with his emphasis on people over production?

The Three Primary Principles of Leadership in the Life of the Leader

Overall, how do we reconcile passages of Scriptures like Luke 19 and Matthew 19:13–14 with Mark 1:29–39 and John 6? How can we maintain that the one and same Messiah would turn aside for Zaccheus and children but leave those seeking healing from physical and demonic ailments in Capernaum and refuse food for those he had fed the day before on the other side of the sea? This question misses the overarching emphasis and why Jesus did what he did. To understand, we have to return to the question of what was God's goal for him. What is his highest commitment?

Revelation 7 offers a picture of a scene in heaven around the eternal throne of God. "After these things I looked, and behold, a great multitude which no one could count, from every nation and all tribes and peoples and tongues, standing before the throne and before the Lamb, clothed in white robes, and palm branches were in their hands; and they cry out with a loud voice, saying, 'Salvation to our God who sits on the throne, and to the Lamb'" (Revelation 7:9–10). Perhaps we could call this passage God's vision statement because it visualizes what God's goal looks like when fulfilled. If this is true, then Matthew 28 is the mission that leads to this consummation. "And Jesus came up and spoke to them, saying, 'All authority has been given to Me in heaven and on earth. Go therefore and make disciples of all the nations, baptizing them in the name of the Father and the Son and the Holy Spirit, teaching them to observe all that I commanded you; and lo, I am with you always, even to the end of the age'" (Matthew 28:18–20). Notice the similar use of language in both passages: "from every nation" and "of all the nations." So what was, and for that matter is, the overarching plan of the Father? His plan is people.

In this plan and mission of God as practiced in the ministry leadership of Jesus, all three primary principles of leadership—having a God goal not simply a good goal, valuing people over production, and never sacrificing the eternal for the temporal—are not only compatible but are also complementary. The reason is that collectively all three principles share and bring about a single focus. God's goal is the eternal redemption of people for his pleasure, glory, and worship for eternity. Therefore, whatever specific form it takes in your ministry, he has called all biblical leaders to the accomplishment of this same mission. All biblical leaders must both understand the dangers of and commit to avoid distractions from simply good goals so they do not neglect God's goal. To understand the calling to biblical leadership fully is to acknowledge that a cursory commitment to making sure we are working toward God's goal is not enough; we must make sure our other activities are not and will not distract from the ultimate mission.

How do we safeguard our focus on and maintain our engagement in this mission? In some ways, the answer to this question is profoundly simple. We must commit to the same three primary principles of leadership observed in the ministry leadership of Jesus. Be willing to sacrifice for the eternal over the call of the temporal. The eternal constitutes the greatest need of people. Be willing to define productivity the way Jesus did. Remember essentially productivity for us relates to the redemption of men's and women's souls as the ultimate task. If a leader understands and practices these two principles, missing the very first principle will be hard if not impossible for him or her: setting aside a good goal in order to choose God's goal, which is the eternal redemption of humankind as the mission.

On the other hand, in many ways, the answer to our question is extremely complex. One reason is the cultural climate and our increasingly complex world has created or brought to light many legitimate needs. Many important ministries and worthy causes exist. These include benevolence and mercy ministries, community care and engagement, and social advocacy and other causes. Many provide valuable opportunities for and support the biblical mission. The leader must engage the church and the individual believer to be aware of all of the biblical precedents for each of these areas. However, our involvement in any one of these good goals must never become a distraction, obstacle, deterrent, or substitute for God's ultimate goal. The reality is if you feed someone, he will become hungry again. If your ministry could heal all the pain, scars, and fears of an abuse victim, she still would need healing in her soul, which only comes from a right relationship with her heavenly Father. Moreover, if the church could become an adequate advocate for every social case, every individual helped is mortal and still must face his or her eternal destination. Yes, engage these issues and your culture, but remember you, your church, and your ministry cannot do everything. Therefore, what you take on must be done with an eye toward the eternal. We must remember God's mission and our ultimate calling as a biblical leader.

In conclusion, then, we should once more consider our working definition of leadership as a model for our leadership practice. How does this description relate to the principles of leadership? And ultimately, how do the principles of leadership affect our leadership for the positive?

The Biblical Definition of Leadership as a Model for Our Practice of Leadership

Notice how much of our working description reflects the three primary principles we have explored in this chapter. "Biblical leadership includes the process of finding God's goal for a specific group of people, instilling that goal in them, equipping them to grow in Christlikeness and fulfill the goal, and empowering them to serve God's eternal kingdom along with you." How does this definition match the three primary principles of leadership? First, holistically it is built around the concept of focusing on and accomplishing God's goal: "finding God's goal for a specific group of people, instilling that goal in them." Second, foundationally it recognizes and values people over production: "equipping them to grow in Christlikeness . . . empowering them." Finally and ultimately, it highlights the eternal nature of our work: "to serve God's eternal kingdom along with you."

How does the perspective serve as a model for positive and effective leadership? A key component of leadership is influence. In fact, Malphurs noted influence as a major component, if not the ultimate aim, of leadership: "Christian leadership is the process whereby servants use their credibility and capability *to influence people* in a particular context to pursue their God-given direction"[64] (emphasis added). He later described influence as "moving people to change their thinking and ultimately their behavior."[65] From chapter 2 of our study, we remember how many experts view influence as the essences of leading. John Maxwell epitomized this approach: *"leadership is influence.* That's it. Nothing more; nothing less"[66] (emphasis added). John MacArthur emphasized the same principle in his definition: "To put it simply, leadership is *influence.* The ideal leader is someone whose life and character motivate people to follow"[67] (emphasis added). Henry Blackaby and Richard Blackaby, using slightly different terminology, affirmed the

---

[64] Malphurs, *Being Leaders*, 10.

[65] Malphurs, 92.

[66] John C. Maxwell, *Developing the Leader Within You* (Nashville: Thomas Nelson, 1993), 1.

[67] John MacArthur, *The Book on Leadership* (Nashville: Thomas Nelson, 2004), vi.

same ideology: "Spiritual leadership is *moving people* on to God's agenda"[68] (emphasis added).

So how much of leadership actually is influence and how important is it to leading? "Influence is the *sine qua non* of leadership, and without it, leadership won't happen."[69] Therefore, the significance of influence to leadership cannot be overstated. If influence is the "must" of leadership, then how can these principles aid and facilitate our leadership impact? In closing, I want to offer three ways the principles of leadership argued for in this chapter strengthen a leader's influence.

First, knowing that the goals of a ministry are indeed biblical goals and that the ultimate mission the leader is pursuing is God's goal will increase followers' potential to follow. People want to be involved in something real, worthwhile, and God-directed. There is a high probability that a genuine believer will want to be a part of what God is doing if she can recognize and understand that God's agenda is the goal.

Second, if you as a leader care about people and are successful in showing them they matter, a higher likelihood exits that they will be persuaded to follow you. Relationships and connections matter to people. If you can then train followers to do the same with others, the probability of your success at influencing increases even more.

Third and perhaps most significantly, being involved in something of eternal importance drives people's interest and commitment. Providing people the opportunity to make a lasting impact can influence them by offering meaning and significance.

---

[68] Henry Blackaby and Richard Blackaby, *Spiritual Leadership: Moving People on to God's Agenda* (Nashville: Broadman and Holman, 2001), 20.
[69] Malphurs, *Being Leaders*, 92

A . . . factor that affects the follower's stage of readiness to follow is the person's sense of self-esteem and significance. If following a leader results in the follower having a sense of personal worth or value, he or she is willing to support the leader and help accomplish the mission. . . . The follower's healthy sense of significance depends in part on whether being involved in a ministry and following its leadership fulfills the desire that his or her life count for Christ. People want to know that they aren't wasting their time. They want to believe that their involvement in ministry is making a difference for the Savior. When people feel that their contribution is important, they make good followers.[70]

Case Study

Now back to Third Baptist Church in Somewhere, America. You were able to work through the leadership characteristic issue with each group. They accepted your plan. Each now believes you are the person to lead, and they are eagerly following you into this new chapter of the church's ministry. As a result, you are making great progress into the process of implementing a new ten-year ministry plan with a strategic focus on evangelism, missions, and disciple making. Within the first five months, however, several different groups approach you about beginning and supplementing the action plan with several other benevolence, community, and advocacy ministries. You believe each of these ministries is biblical and would provide great opportunities for and supplements to the ministry at some point in the future. You, however, have two immediate concerns. First, the church has not had a real discipleship focus in years. Its tendency in the past has been to get easily distracted from the biblical mission by almost anything and everything else. You have a

---

[70] Malphurs, 125.

genuine feeling that this could happen again with any of these ministries, especially in the current state of the congregation. Second, right now you are not sure whether the church has the volunteer and leadership base to staff one, let alone all, of these ministries. The overall thrust of the new ten-year plan is essentially going to require all hands on deck if it has any chance of success.

How do you address these concerns in a productive way while maintaining the positive momentum you have gained? Specifically, how do you keep and perhaps increase your ability to influence followers and safeguard your church's focus and engagement on the biblical goal? Write a detailed plan as to how you would build the practice of leadership in response to this scenario. Be specific, and be sure to include support as to why this is your chosen path. You may supplement your answer with other information and sources, but be sure to include information from our study in chapter 6, especially as it relates to the three primary principles of biblical leadership.

Chapter 7

Managing the Work

The art of management involves rearranging ministry work for maximum productivity toward accomplishing the corporate vision and mission. Anything we commit to work toward means we have said no to something else. We have to forecast the future based on what we can manage effectively without merely developing a "field of dreams" mentality.[71] Management is an ongoing evaluation and planning so church programs reach maximum effectiveness.

All churches have busier seasons than others, but some allow the work to cascade into an unmanageable church calendar. There are days I desire a few extra hours of uninterrupted office time to complete remaining tasks, which leaves me feeling accomplished and satisfied with my efforts. Robert Fryling stated, "Our work as leaders is never done and because work can be addictive, it is easy to lose boundaries. . . . We morph from being effective in leading others to being exhausted in being led by the demands of

---

[71] *Field of Dreams* is a 1989 movie starring Kevin Costner as Ray Kinsella. Standing in the middle of his cornfield, Ray hears a voice saying, "If you build it, he will come." Ray and his family risk their farm to build a baseball field with the expectation that standout players from history will arrive to play.

others."[72] How do we manage everything in our ministry to ensure we are staying healthy to love God with all our heart, mind, soul, and strength? We also need to love our family, neighbors, and others around us. In the Gospel of John, Jesus said, "Peace I leave with you. My peace I give to you. I do not give to you as the world gives. Don't let your heart be troubled or fearful" (14:27 CSB). Managing the work helps us develop a rhythm for life and ministry, undergirded by the peace given through Jesus Christ.

We all have the same number of hours each week, but how we spend that time is crucial to what we achieve. In my years of service to churches of varying sizes, I've had similar conversations. Whether with a businessperson, parent, or minister, the sentiment is generally the same: "I just don't feel like I am doing anything well." I've also heard, "I just don't have enough days or hours to get it all accomplished." Rarely does anyone share their ability to accomplish everything they desire. There are days I recount similar statements in my own mind during seasons with busy schedules and overwhelming responsibilities. Management is the key to peace and thriving contrasted with others whose daily cadence is pushed, hurried, and unsettled.

Managing the work has become more challenging as we have more information than ever to navigate. We also stay connected to more people through social media networks and advancing technology. Thus, the problems and information have simply increased at a pace our minds have a hard time processing. In ministry, this challenge is compounded by our care for people who are hurting and in physical or spiritual need. Ministry provides a unique challenge in management. Whether you lead a small group, pastor a church, or serve on a leadership team or committee, the challenge to manage

---

[72] Robert A. Fryling, *The Leadership Ellipse: Shaping How We Lead by Who We Are* (Downers Grove, IL: IVP Books, 2010), 118.

all things well can be stressful. Managing growing, maturing disciples of Jesus Christ is a difficult task. To avoid being overwhelmed, we have to assess and assign value to each activity or person in which we invest. For most of us, this is a task in time management.

In ministry, we must first take stock of our personal calendar. To manage the work, we should take an inventory of each activity, person, and responsibility that requires our attention. Next, we move to the ministry calendar and begin to review those responsibilities. It is important to differentiate good from necessary. A full calendar does not equate with a well-managed life. When not enough attention is given to the right things, then a strategic decision must be made—which activities should remain on the calendar and which ones are unnecessary? The writer of Proverbs reminds ministry leaders, "Where there is no vision, the people perish" (29:18 KJV). A well-stated mission and vision are key guideposts for determining the priority of each calendar event.

Another leadership challenge is determining parameters for work. This often requires a strategic shift to only commit to primary ministries and the difficult task of saying no to good things. "Without God's people leading according to God's design, a culture will inevitably deteriorate. Culture in church, home, and the workplace will self-destruct without God's people distributing His grace through their leadership. We must be leaders and develop leaders who reflect, replicate, and cultivate."[73]

This begs the question, when do you stop doing something? One of the most challenging tasks I have encountered over the years is to begin eliminating some events and programs for ministry. Elimination of nonessential programs and events is an important part of

---

[73] Eric Geiger and Kevin Peck, *Designed to Lead: The Church and Leadership Development* (Nashville: Broadman and Holman, 2016), 73.

management. Many congregations have been conditioned to believe the events and programs are vital to the church. However, everything we agree to do takes time, talent, and treasure to achieve. Excellent management is able to discern the priority and precedence each event or program deserves, including considering volunteer hours, personal giftedness, financial resources, and facility availability. Wise management can achieve a shift in the mindset of congregants from being programmatic to mission-driven. Mission-driven management drives spiritual growth in the local church.

Let's also think about the opposite scenario. When do you add a new ministry to support the mission and vision? When you start the process of strategically managing the work, you may peel back the layers and discover biblical mandates being overlooked, such as the groups of widows who have been left out in the distribution of food.[74] Of equal importance to excellent management is ensuring biblical commands are included in the essential work of the local church. There is a process for managing the work to add to the work strategically, which is covered in a later chapter.

Tips: Managing the Work

Most churches do not offer a blank canvas for leadership and planning. Even as a new pastor, you often spend your first months in ministry determining how a God-given vision fits with the current rhythm and church calendar. I would suggest an important first step is assessing the costs of both time and talent for events and programs. How many hours and people does it take for a specific event or program?

---

[74] See Acts 6.

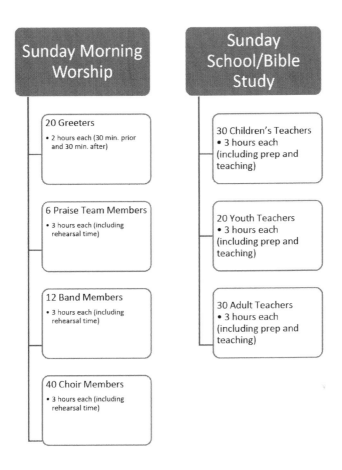

Sunday Morning Worship

20 Greeters
- 2 hours each (30 min. prior and 30 min. after)

6 Praise Team Members
- 3 hours each (including rehearsal time)

12 Band Members
- 3 hours each (including rehearsal time)

40 Choir Members
- 3 hours each (including rehearsal time)

Sunday School/Bible Study

30 Children's Teachers
- 3 hours each (including prep and teaching)

20 Youth Teachers
- 3 hours each (including prep and teaching)

30 Adult Teachers
- 3 hours each (including prep and teaching)

Time and Talent Considerations for Managing the Work

This diagram is an example of time and talent considerations for an average Sunday morning worship setting. Seeing the necessary people and hours in a diagram undergirds the enormous investment to manage. When you multiply people by time (20 greeters x 2 hours = 40 hours), this Sunday morning setup requires 214 volunteer hours. Likewise, the Sunday school setup in the diagram above requires 240 volunteer hours. Suddenly, serving on the praise team or teaching Sunday school isn't an "easy" responsibility; it's an essential aspect of a major plan to see the local church develop mature disciples of Jesus Christ.

In ministry, it is easy to get caught in the "field of dreams" rut; if I build it, copy it, or reinvent it, then we will grow again and be back to where we need to be as a church. The calendar can be full of events that then keep your people busy but not engaged in a discipleship pathway, creating mature followers of Jesus Christ. Another essential aspect of managing the work is learning to coach our people well. Moving beyond details of the work toward investing and equipping the team should be a priority for ministry leaders. An effective coach prepares and equips the team for game time, relying on previous work or other leaders to handle details, such as water and first aid.

The struggle is real because each day is unpredictable. Proverbs 27:1 reminds us, "Don't boast about tomorrow, / for you don't know what a day might bring" (CSB). We know the Lord appoints our days and has a plan of how we should focus our attention for each of those days. He is the creator, and as a result we can only extend our life by focusing how we live on him. In Proverbs 3 we are exhorted to keep the teaching of God's commands because it will bring us "many days, a full life, and well-being" (vv. 1–2). We have choices along the way in areas of our lives like whether or not we respond to authority with respect or how we choose to treat those around us. As leaders we must manage each aspect of the ministry without always knowing what challenges or new opportunities the week or year may bring.

So as we pivot, the focus of the work moves from managing to walking with the Lord, relating to others, and getting the work done that he has called us to accomplish. In any given week we can let our rhythm accelerate to a tempo we cannot keep pace with or we can be so slow that we are not as productive as we could be. I remember when I first got married the shift in my rhythm of how I spent my days and weeks now involved another person 24/7. This shift was easier with my workflow because we did many things together surrounding ministry and the church. The hardest shift was when I became a dad. My rhythm did not reflect availability for the family, and I was starting doctoral work while being in a growing church that had steadily increasing demands and challenges. I found myself burning the candle at both ends. My family suffered because I was not as present and available as I needed to be, but ultimately I was not a healthy follower of Christ as a result of the demanding schedule. As long as I could hold it together and could manage the work, then the church was satisfied with my work and not concerned with my health and family. I had to realize that if I did not adjust, then all could be lost. The COVID-19 pandemic was a reminder of this fact as well. I learned the following truth as a child: "For what does it benefit someone to gain the whole world and yet lose his life?" (Mark 8:36). Managing the workflow so that the people are growing in Christ, overseeing the details of ministry, and advancing the mission without anyone being consumed by the workload is a challenging but necessary pursuit.

Ministry can be an ongoing season of change due to expectations or needs of the people. Basketball players learn to pivot as they move the ball toward the basket. In ministry we have to adapt or pivot to be in the best position possible for what the Lord has for us. We should be continually looking at how we can adjust so that mission achievement is attainable. We have to be willing to adapt with the changing conditions around us in order to compete. You have read in Paul's writings about conditioning yourself to be able to compete at the highest level of skill and endurance that is possible. Since the conditions are imposed upon us beyond our control, we should expect ministry to cause us to have to adapt. A couple of points to consider:

> ➤ What are the easiest adaptations for you to accept in your life and ministry?
> ➤ If you struggle to adapt, then pause, consider, and pray as to why you have difficulty.

Change is hard and the constant pressure to keep the plates spinning can be overwhelming for leaders. The unrelenting weight can sink us as ministry leaders, so take time to be sure you are growing in your pursuit of Christ. The overall picture of Jesus's ministry was adapting his methods to minister to the crowds or interact one on one with someone on their journey. When we consider adapting, the process does not have to be negative. Pause and pray that your ministry mission becomes more like Jesus while also following his example of being a person who walks with God.

I know you may be reading the first several chapters and thinking that managing the work is consuming. You may even be on the verge of burnout or quitting. When I got sick with an illness that landed me in bed for longer than a week, I was faced with the reality that life is not a guarantee. I grew up with that perspective having lost my father at a young age and having infant siblings who never left the hospital. I began to ponder, *If this is the end, have I invested my life in the right things?* As I pondered day after day wondering what was next and if life would continue, I asked myself these questions: Have I loved those around me? Have I shared the gospel and made disciples as commanded by Jesus? Have I lived selflessly for him in the areas he called me, or have I lived for myself? These driving questions make us evaluate life. I did not desire to manage my email folder, the facility, the alignment of the weekly programs, or another special event. Some weeks we have to plan the event, deal with a facility issue, or navigate a conflict, but the overall management of ministry will eventually cause burnout if a plan for coping with the ongoing demands is not implemented.

Managing People, Programs, and Facilities

Managing the people of ministry can be overwhelming, but the church is the people. As you and I minister, we need to coach and mentor more than we strive to manage, placing our priority on people above programs and facilities. Managing people will be an ongoing element of your ministry. There will always be challenges: the senior adult who posts their grievances on social media, a member who complains when they are trying to express concerns, or members who don't have effective communication skills. Any given week, a team member will be walking through a life crisis, and we have to make room in our schedule to listen, encourage, pray for, and help guide. As we strive to be wise managers, we have to be committed to loving and investing in the people who we have the opportunity to disciple.

Even when prioritizing people, you still have to manage the programs, calendar, facility, and budget. However, these will not matter as much if you do not invest in the people first. Managing helps a leader earn the right to lead in the more critical areas of ministry. If a facility is not clean, the programs are dysfunctional, and the budget is never balanced, each decision will be evaluated at a higher level by the people who support the church. Lay leaders and staff have to lead well in managing the details so that the major ministry components are successful and propel the church toward their mission and vision. If mismanagement happens, people begin to question leadership, and the ministry suffers. And thus the church suffers. Again, an organizational mission and vision provide a framework for decision making that helps leaders make wise decisions.

Programs are defined as any ministry activity focused on the activities within and through a local congregation. Time allows for many programs to be started because someone or a group of people have an idea, attend a conference, or desire to duplicate a plan from another ministry.

> Programs that fit within the church's vision and mission are great, but the problem is when programs determine the vision or mission.

Every good idea is not an essential idea. Each church has a capacity for how much they can accomplish. One can choose to partner with another church, choose not to add another good idea, or acknowledge the need but let another church take on a program that can add to what it is already doing. Just as in your personal life, you must determine the priority of each opportunity. Thus, the church does not have enough managing capacity to say yes to every program option available.

Any ministry will benefit from having a system for calendaring the church and events for consistency. Systems allow for managing the facilities, people, and overall ministry plan for making disciples. I believe in having systems for the crucial aspects of managing ministry. Tony Morgan, in his book, *The Unstuck Church*, identifies six common characteristics for healthy systems:

1. Healthy systems empower leaders to accomplish ministry without always having to get permission.
2. Healthy systems are embraced and championed by the top leadership.
3. Healthy systems mobilize more people rather than lean on a handful of talented individuals.
4. Healthy systems simplify the path.

5. Healthy systems improve over time.

6. Healthy systems need to change over time.[75]

I encourage you to find a system that supports your ministry context and the corporate priorities you've chosen. Insist that the ministry teams use the same or similar systems so planning across the leadership team is consistent and systematic. Make time each year for review and discussion of systems so your ministry maintains maximum efficiency.

Another part of systems management includes facilities. Some churches have large facilities that require ongoing maintenance while others rely on rented or shared space with minimal upkeep. Facilities can be a costly component to our church and ministry budgets. A healthy system for managing your facilities will significantly benefit your work, allowing fiscal resources to be allocated appropriately.

Volunteer management ensures local ministry has a group of people committed to getting the work done. Volunteers need a system to be recruited, trained, and deployed to serve. Part of volunteerism includes first impressions, where people are greeted upon arrival and connected to the church ministries and activities. Many churches forget to consider a system for developing this vital component of connecting new people. A system of management can relieve the stress of ongoing volunteer recruitment for ministry leaders, ensuring continuing ministry of the local church.

Questions for Reflection

1. What is your ministry mission and vision? Do your mission and vision provide structure for managing the work of the church?

---

[75] Tony Morgan, *The Unstuck Church: Equipping Churches to Experience Sustained Health* (Nashville: Thomas Nelson, 2017), 76.

2. What systems does your church have?

3. What systems do you need to consider developing?

4. What aspects of managing the work come naturally for you?

5. What components of the work overwhelm or are a struggle for you?

Case Study

It was a busy Sunday morning because we just moved to town, but we decided to get the kids ready and make our way to a church we located through a Google search. We arrived with our two kids but were unsure which direction to go from the parking lot. Since it was not our first time visiting a church, we took a guess and headed inside. After entering, we learned that the times on the website did not match the actual times for Sunday morning worship. Since we are pretty flexible, we rolled with the time change. Friendly people greeted us, but no one offered to guide us through participating that day at church or directing us through the facility. Was there an order of service? What about childcare for our baby?

We survived the first Sunday and decided to try again the next week. Since we had been Christ followers for several years, we desired to be a part of a church that valued membership and offered opportunities for involvement and service. No one helped us when we inquired about becoming a part of the church and serving. So we found ourselves at a crossroads: Why did no one desire for us to become a part of their faith family?

What part of the work might have been overlooked in managing this local church?

What systems could help this church manage a better Sunday morning experience for this family?

Chapter 8
Making Sense of the Structure

As a leader you need to understand the structure of church staff, volunteers, programs, and ministries, including how to align each element within the larger church structure. Understanding structure provides a foundation for planning meetings, building ministry teams and committees, and identifying necessary resources to lead the ministry forward. Structure also includes guiding documents such as bylaws, policies, and procedures that reflect essential functions. Considering the working systems within the church will enable efficiency and accountability for both oversight and governance.

Hopefully, you do not look at your ministry or church each week and think you are "building this plane in the air." This statement has become more common as leaders discuss the challenges of organizational structures in a rapidly evolving world. Throughout the Bible, we are given instruction for worship, governing people, relating to one another through a local congregation, avoiding false doctrine, and dealing with those who are not repentant or cause division within the church, among many other things. Yet some of the legal and structural aspects of a healthy church are not mentioned in scripture. Thankfully, other biblical principles are available to develop a foundation for the structure of a local church and deal with our ministry's business components.

Church Structure: Foundational Elements

Some ministers and laypeople have adapted business principles and strategies to their church structure. Some have simply struggled within an inherited ministry framework from another generation of leadership. Regardless of the circumstances, a church structure should have similar, foundational aspects in place—a constitution, bylaws, a policy and procedure manual, and an overall organizational outline for staff and volunteers. One key aspect of navigating a changing culture is to have a clear doctrinal understanding of the collective local church beliefs and the members' responsibilities. Many factors of how a church constitutes itself and what it believes about God and the Bible determines the structure's next aspects. The local church and its ethos are foundational aspects of local ministry and require consideration before adopting systems from other organizations. Each church has a unique ethos, and every community has some nuances to how they function as a local church body. Let's take a closer look at some structural elements for the local church.

When making sense of the structure, three things are essential: prayer, a review of the organizational history, and a revision or drafting of the documents that will guide and direct the church's structure. In consulting with churches to help them make sense of their structure as they respond to problems or adapt to their changing needs, I often encounter similar circumstances. A few people feel their opinions should carry more weight due to family ties, history of giving, or church politics. Some churches are unwilling to make sense of their structure and are happy if the church just limps along. I believe a desire for excellence in executing the local church's mission demonstrates a vibrant witness for Christ, reflecting his son's work while on earth.

The larger a congregation becomes, the more the structure will expand to support the work and the resources needed to have a reliable local ministry structure. The specific church size will determine some aspects of the structure, and as a result, the following church sizes will guide the various components that comprise the church's structure.

Robert Welch stated, "Any organization needs documents that define what it is and its mission and purpose, the structure by which it will do business, and the process that directs activity."[76] These documents need a straightforward process for being adopted and how they can be adapted or revised as needed. For example, many guiding documents did not allow for virtual meetings in place of in-person meetings—an adaptation that has since become vital.

For this administrative structure discussion, various church sizes are considered with some generalizations pertinent to each:

Church Size: Under 100

Churches of fewer than 100 in average worship attendance operate more organically with a few families that influence most decisions. Often in the smaller congregations the attention to documents and processes has been left to how key people desire to handle the church's business. We must remember that church size is not a factor in property liability, people, and processes. Regardless of numeric attendance, attention to structural documents provides stability for the local church family.

---

[76] Robert H. Welch, *Church Administration: Creating Efficiency for Effective Ministry* (Nashville: B&H Academic, 2005), 51.

Church Size: 101–250

This size can be one of the hardest to manage because it is more extensive but still has a core group of influential families. The church has grown to have more ministries and enough people that the structure is still family in nature but requires more people to be involved. The church's overall health will be guided by clear guidelines that let the church focus on ministry and not always in committee or business meetings. One of the struggles for a congregation as it conducts the work based on its structure will require it to have a time-management consideration of how much time people have to meet and organize the work of business and ministry. In a culture with busy schedules, making allowance for virtual attendance in committee or team meetings can be vital to keeping the work moving forward.

Church Size: 250–500, 501–999, and 1,000 or more

These are the church size categories that shift some of the guiding leadership documents and structures within a congregation. In a larger church, the documents become more of a staff-led structure than a committee-led structure that involves a different relationship among the following areas. However, each church has to determine a structure that allows it to state who it is, why it exists, what it believes, where it is located, who composes the membership, and how it is governed.

Another point of consideration should be if the church is established with these structures and has been declining, then at what church-size metric do the structure and documents need to change. The reverse is also true as a church grows: how do the structure and guiding documents need to change to allow for the church's clarity and the business aspects that need a straightforward decision-making process? Like Welch, I believe any church needs three committees: property, personnel, and finance. Churches must also consider their legal trustees who help oversee the big picture of borrowing money, executing contracts, and liability exposure to the church's work.

Constitution and Bylaws

Every church should have a constitution and bylaws that speak to the church's current structure and situation. A Church constitution states the "definitive . . . name, location, doctrinal purpose, and rules of conduct of the church. It is the way the organization is structured. It includes basic beliefs, dogma, and polity. It describes the covenant under which the membership operates."[77] Bylaws should be a concise document that

> focus on the rights and privileges of the members, the responsibilities and powers of church officers and how they become officers as well as how long they will serve. Included in the bylaws are rules for doing business and conducting meetings, who will moderate meetings, and the parameters for quorum. Committees and other polity organizations of the body are identified. How finances are received and used is defined.[78]

A church can also be incorporated as a nonprofit organization. I recommend any church consider filing with their state to be a stand-alone incorporated organization recognized as a church.

---

[77] Welch, 52.
[78] Welch.

Policies and Procedures

Policies and procedures should only be articulated when and if they are intended to be implemented and utilized. These are the best places to state personnel, property, and financial details of the organization and the overall details and administrative details for executing these three primary areas of executive function within the church. Personnel policies and procedures should detail time off, hiring processes, sick leave, and other typical office management information. Property policies and procedures should include the ongoing concerns with facility use and care and processes for ongoing maintenance needs. Financial policies and procedures should cover the fiscal method for accounting for income, the process for disbursing funds, and how it will account for designated monies. Many churches defer the maintenance to save money, but the building will continue to deteriorate without an investment, just like our private residences.

The policy and procedure manual should be a fluid, ongoing document that can be easily updated. You need a process for adding or removing items. If you have a committee for each of these three critical areas—personnel, property, and financial—they can oversee that specific area's policies and procedures. As the personnel, property, or finance team encounters an area of their work that needs to be edited for current practice, you can deal with the concerns and have an ongoing working document that serves the church and its people.

Organizational Structure

Organizational structures should consider when a staff member should be assigned or hired to oversee an area of ministry, when a committee needs to make recommendations and decisions for an area of the church, or when a ministry team is necessary to oversee and guide a specific component of ministry. Many types of structures can be observed from a hierarchal to a decentralized relationship structure. The most critical aspect of choosing a church structure is deciding what works for your church context and the people working within your local ministry. Church structure may morph as your leadership matures or changes or the church's needs develop over time. You need to adopt a functional structure that works for your people and addresses their needs to have access to leadership and decisions made in a timely process.

> The overall process for leadership and guiding documents is intended to help a church navigate conflict and conduct business legally and ethically.

There will be challenges throughout the leadership and administration structures of any church. An organization structure should be established that clarifies the decision-making process, so when conflict or challenges arise that need to be dealt with, the process is in place and clearly defined. Churches have organic relationships and connections that makes business-type decisions a challenge as people share information. A formal system that demonstrates pertinent details with each decision provides accountability and clarity to keep the ministry moving forward.

Church Membership

Church membership guidelines have to be explained and followed to have an accurate account of who constitutes the church's membership. Each church has to articulate in their bylaws who can be members, how one becomes a member, and how one is removed from the membership. The church needs to take this aspect seriously because membership should mean something to the people. A clear understanding of church membership and the members' rights and responsibilities should be addressed so people understand expectations as they choose to request membership.

Church Dissolution

Plans for dissolution is not an area many consider because they cannot grasp a future in which the local church they are an active participant in would ever cease to exist. Any church should have a plan for the process of dissolution. I have passed large and small church buildings that no longer have a congregation gathering each week for worship. Each organization should have a straightforward process for donating the assets in dissolving so that ministry continues through the property or funds.

Partnerships

Partnerships should be considered in light of the doctrinal beliefs of the church. A few considerations should be deliberated as a church partners with other organizations, entities, and communities. Most churches are committed to partnering with a regional association for the cooperative work in their area for missions, benevolence, and other ministry areas. Another partnership may be with a denomination at a state or national level. A church may also consider partnership with a ministry for a retreat, camp, and branding and curriculum.

Many ministry organizations exist that coach on leadership, media components, conferences, and networks. Any church should consider their partnerships and understand the philosophy and direction of groups with whom they partner. In a community, a church should think about outside organizations such as Boy Scouts, Girl Scouts, school districts, and nonprofit groups to be sure the ways you partner are in agreement with your guiding documents for the church's doctrine and mission. Suppose these groups do not agree in these ways. In that case, the group is not a partner but a person who needs to rent the facility if a church is open to leasing or allowing a partner to contract the use of the facilities even if money does not change hands.

Insurance

Insurance is an aspect that can cover every part of your ministry. Most churches have liability and property insurance. Many types of coverage exist within these two broad areas of insurance. In the liability arena, a general umbrella liability is what I describe as the tent of coverage, under which every aspect of liability could fit. Five parts need to be understood within an insurance policy: declarations, definitions, exclusions, conditions, and the insurance agreement. These are the foundational aspects of insurance so you can understand what your policies cover or how to vet your insurance company and types of coverage. I recommend consulting the following when dealing with insurance: GuideOne, Brotherhood Mutual, and Church Mutual. These three insurers specialize in churches and provide free resources to help you in church safety and administration for your congregations.

Church Property and Facilities

Property is a component of every church's structure because you own, borrow, or rent space to have a place to meet. Area is a crucial aspect because it can be the most expensive piece to ministry in the Western world. If you rent, then I suggest you have experts review the rental contract to understand the terms and conditions for what you agree to and any expectations for maintenance and facility usage observed during the agreement's time frame. If you own your property, then a plan for ongoing maintenance has to be followed. Each church needs policies and procedures for their property. Weddings, funerals, church events, community events, and private functions are examples of property usage types. Each type will need to be cleaned, safe, and secure, but each varies according to the church's mission.

Your church facility should be clean concerning the floors, bathrooms, trash, and overall aspects of the property after each scheduled activity. The outdoor property, such as the landscaping, upkeep, cleanliness, and general cosmetic look of your church, is an area you need to always consider for people's safety and aesthetic appeal. You may not be able to afford new facilities, but everyone can have a clean, well-kept, inviting building. We all choose to conduct business each week with people and places based on how a restaurant or retail location looks or smells. As you consider your space, think about a family and whether your children's area is as lovely as a local daycare or the elementary school. Consider the student space and whether teenagers desire to be in an environment like the one you cultivate. Adults do not appreciate second-rate space either, and a fresh coat of paint and some cleaning can go a long way in changing the atmosphere of your ongoing ministry and improve your facility's look.

Trustees or officers—the people who have the legal authority to act on behalf of the organization—must be defined. A process for selection and replacement for these positions should be clarified in the guiding documents. Be sure the active list aligns with the businesses and legal documents of your organization, as these individuals are the church's legal signatures. I have consulted with churches that stated a desire to update their policies and procedures manual, but then never followed them. Another church had officers and trustees still listed on banking accounts from decades prior who no longer even attended the church.

Systems and Documents

Systems can be helpful in the overall work of the church. You should consider always having a system for financial bookkeeping and records as well as for the membership directory. These two systems can be used within some church software systems to handle both or most of your overall data needs. You may also consider a digital check-in system for guests and minors as well as a security system for your facility. In the ongoing work of the church, you may find other systems to be helpful to you. It is essential to consider how you will schedule your facility, volunteers, and programs in the church's ongoing work. You will find a system that will help ensure you have not double-booked a building, a volunteer, or ministry to support your church's ongoing work. I have found the best advice in this area by always being a student of what others are doing and looking for ways to continue to improve.

Administrative documents, structures, and processes are not the items that usually excite us for ministry, but they are helpful when they are in place and keep the church working efficiently. When problems occur—because there will be problems—then a well-developed organization can weather the crisis better than one that is disorganized. Leaders who have done the hard work of developing systems and processes have shared how thankful they were to already have a plan in place when a challenge arose. Many churches defer the maintenance to save money, but the building will continue to deteriorate without an investment, just like our private residences. You do not want to achieve an unhealthy balance in your people, property, or finances. As the world continues to turn to digital means, you should consider options for your guiding documents. If you still have paper documents on file, consider scanning them as digital copies and backing them up digitally so they are never lost within your facility or in a file that another person cannot find.

Conclusion

Structures will always be fluid and change as organizations grow and decline and people come and go. As you consider your structure, do not think it will last a lifetime, but look with the vision and mission in mind. Be sure your system will help you move forward with the goals and objectives you have in place to reach and make disciples and carry out the primary functions of the local church. The structure can be adapted as you move forward and should be developed in a way that it can expand—or shrink—as needed. In ministry, it is easy to work hard to get all the structure pieces created or updated and then forget them, but the ongoing challenge is to keep these pieces current to the church's relevant needs. In a litigious society, these pieces of our structure are more important and more scrutinized than ever. We do not plan that a new minister will turn out to be a bad fit and then need a process for removal. The thought of an assistant being a thief is hard to grasp. The volunteer that treats all the church resources as their own is not a problem until something is needed and cannot be found. The list of what-if stories could be extended, and I have heard many real-life horror stories of things that happen when the structure is not established and followed.

A healthy structure that fits the ethos of the congregation that allows for the organization to grow and remain viable is crucial. When things are going well, people will question these items less, but people begin to scrutinize them when challenges are evident. Many factors will guide the direction of a church and its ministries, members, and business. These documents, processes, and relationships should be in place. Through its leadership, a church continues to update and evaluate how these are working through the lens of the church and its relationship with the people, church's partnerships, relationships within the community, and compliance with government as deemed appropriate through the doctrinal statements of the church. Wisdom and flexibility are needed during a crisis, whether death, a pandemic, natural disasters, or other unexpected catastrophic events. When we face an unexpected turn of events, the guiding documents help us navigate the crisis with a clear plan. We will not always have the answers and will need to adapt as unique challenges arise. We can rely on the structure to help us know a direction or process that our people will understand. A leader who can show the rationale and how it followed the church-approved procedures is always better than when everyone has an opinion.

Case Study

During the first quarter of the year, the church has been growing, but a few families are not sure of the overall direction. As they begin to talk to one another, they question the budget, a new ministry that has been created, and whether the minister works enough hours. Their thoughts simmer over the coming days and weeks. The church is looking toward a new horizon as the quarterly business meeting is scheduled. The reality is nothing has been done outside of the guidelines of the church, yet several members seem disconnected and don't understand the reason behind church decisions. What systems or structures could a church have to stop these disgruntled members before it becomes a significant issue?

Discussion Questions

1. Does your ministry have guiding documents? When is the last time your guiding documents were reviewed?

2. What is your organizational structure? Why did you choose this particular structure?

3. How can your facility be improved? What small projects could create the biggest impact? Likewise, what larger projects are necessary for continued growth?

4. Which areas do you have a good process for the administrative work?

5. How do you utilize systems in your ministry?

Chapter 9

Facilitating Change

"Change is inevitable." This axiom is true in all of life. It also is true in the home, business, and practically every aspect of society. In church and ministry leadership, change is certain as well. I am not sure who first made this statement or when I first heard it, but I know I have found the reality of change to be true during my time serving churches and God's kingdom. A leader must be ready to both manage and lead change in his or her ministry as well.

We have seen the importance of both who a leader is (the person of leadership) and what a leader does (the practice of leadership). When the person of leadership and the practice of leadership are guided by solid and consistent principles, you can, and perhaps will, have influence with followers. Moreover, much of leadership and its significance is described, understood, and recognized by influence (see chapter 2).

However, the question that naturally follows this logical progression is once you have this influence, what do you do with it? In other words, why does influence matter for a leader? Perhaps the answer to this question is that influence matters for most, if not all, activities in which a leader engages. However, remember the opening statement to this chapter: change is inevitable. If this saying is indeed true, a person cannot be a leader without being affected by and thus needing to lead change. Leaders live in a perpetually changing world and are responsible for facilitating change in both their worlds and the worlds of their followers. Therefore, how can managing and affecting change be accomplished successfully? Is there a biblical mandate or support for doing so? And, more importantly, can change be led successfully and the leader survive?

In this chapter, we will consider an eight-step strategy for ministry leaders to facilitate change in the local church and other ministry contexts. We will begin by examining the biblical precedent and need for change in the local church and ministry settings. Next, we will explore the actual eight-step strategy, which takes into consideration our definition of and approach to biblical leadership. Finally, we will consider two practical factors in ministry leadership that are important when implementing the eight-step change strategy.

Biblical Foundation for the Necessity of Change in Ministry Leadership

A general overview of the New Testament Epistles lends credence to the idea that change is inevitable in the church and provides a biblical precedent for leading change in ministry. Consider how many of Paul's thirteen letters identified a problem that needed correction and thus a change that needed to be made. Even instances in which the primary purpose of his writing was making an appeal for change, Paul addressed the need for change or called for a course correction in at least some portion of most of his letters. These calls for changes range from those very practical in nature (i.e., 1 Corinthians, 1 Thessalonians, and Ephesians) to those that address significant doctrinal issues (i.e., Romans, Galatians, and Colossians).

For our purposes here, however, we will consider a section of text in which Christ addressed several of his churches about the need for change. The passage in question is Revelation 2 and 3. In only two chapters of the Bible and of the seven churches that are addressed, at least five are in need of a major shift in the life and direction of the congregation and thus are called to significant change. The concerns range from the loss of a close relationship with the Lord and the fruit, which is born from that relationship, to the departure from doctrinal purity and personal purity and finally to the acceptance of a self-sufficient perspective leading to congregational uselessness. In each instance, a metaphor is used that could, and in some cases does, lead to debate over details and specifics. However, one thing is clear. Each of these five churches needed a course correction, a change if you will.

First, after complimenting it for several admirable aspects of its congregational life, including its doctrinal fidelity, Christ rebuked the Ephesian church for leaving its "first love" (Revelation 2:4). The church is called to repent (v. 5), that is to change course. At least four views for the interpretation, or more specifically the identification, of its "first love" have been suggested. These range from love of Christ to love of other believers to love of Christ and other believers to love of Christ, other believers, and unbelievers.[79] The two most prominent and probable are love for Christ and other believers or a love for Christ, including an application for the unbeliever.

The former perspective was represented and taken by R. C. H. Lenski. "The love here mentioned is not only love to the brethren, for this love and the love to Christ are never

---

[79] Ronald L. Trail, *An Exegetical Summary of Revelation 1-11*, 2nd ed. (Dallas: SIL International, 2008), 49.

separate, the former is the evidence for the latter (1 John 4:20)."[80] The latter was held and explained by G. K. Beale:

> Although they were ever on guard to maintain the purity of the apostolic teaching, the Ephesian Christians were not diligent in witnessing to the same faith in the outside world (the content of apostolic doctrine must be defined by the context of the Apocalypse and the NT itself; cf. 1 Cor. 15:1–4). This is what is meant when Christ chastises them for having left their "first love." The point is not primarily that they had lost their love for one another, as argued by most commentators (e.g., Moffatt's translation, "you have given up loving one another as you did at first"). Nor is the point merely that they had lost their love for Christ in general (as some commentators also think; cf. Jer. 2:2; Ezek. 16:8). The idea is that they no longer expressed their former zealous love for Jesus *by witnessing to him in the world.*[81]

Regardless, we know that this church lay in some state of a spiritual coldness in or distance from its relationship to and thus service for Jesus, even though it had preserved right doctrine. It needed a change.

The second and third examples of the churches that need correction appear to be more straightforward, at least as relating to the general nature of the problems. Both churches had failed to deal with the presence and ministries of false teachers among them. The church in Pergamum appears to have *only* accepted false teachers and thus their false teachings at this point. "You have there some who hold the teaching of Balaam, who kept teaching Balak to put a stumbling block

---

[80] R. C. H. Lenski, *The Interpretation of St. John's Revelation* (Minneapolis: Augsburg, 1963), 86.

[81] G. K. Beale, *The Book of Revelation: A Commentary on the Greek Text,* The New International Greek Testament Commentary (Grand Rapids: William B. Eerdmans; Carlisle, Cumbria: Paternoster Press, 1999), 230.

before the sons of Israel, to eat things sacrificed to idols and to commit acts of immorality. So you also have some who in the same way hold the teaching of the Nicolaitans" (Revelation 2:14–15). The church in Thyatira, however, had fallen into a much more dire state. Not only had it tolerated a false teacher, but its acceptance of false doctrine actually had led to at least some instances of impure living. "You tolerate the woman Jezebel, who calls herself a prophetess, and she teachers and leads My bond-servants astray so that they commit acts of immorality and eat things sacrificed to idols. . . . Behold, I will throw her on a bed of sickness, and those who commit adultery with her into great tribulation, unless they repent of her deeds" (vv. 20, 22). Both churches were called to change direction (vv. 16, 22).

Fourth, the church in Sardis was teetering on the precipice of utter disaster. As a result, the Lord gave a stern warning to "wake up," seemingly imploring the church to be aware and cautious concerning its nearness to the edge of destruction (Revelation 3:2). But what exactly was the problem in this fellowship? An outward appearance not matching an inward reality may have been its downfall (v. 1). "In Sardis the question is the relationship between reputation and reality. The reputation of the church at Sardis was life, but the reality was that they were dead."[82] Therefore, either the church members had become apathetic in their life with Christ, not maintaining their discipleship, or they only had an appearance of spiritual life in the first place (vv. 3–4). "The Church had the name *Christian* church, but its Christian life was dying inwardly: 'thou art dead,' thou as a church."[83] As to the exact nature of the problem, three views are possible: a loss of a zeal for evangelism that would eventually lead to a

---

[82] Paige Patterson, *Revelation*, The New American Commentary, vol. 39 (Nashville: B&H, 2012), 121.

[83] Lenski, *Interpretation of St. John's Revelation*, 127.

total death of the congregation, numerical health but spiritual death, or an acceptance of false teaching and thus doctrinal death.[84] Determining which of these theories is correct may be impossible, but the departure from evangelism is worth considering. Had their problem affected their witness for the kingdom of God and thus produced a state much like the one described in Ephesus? "Likewise the *so-called* Christians of Sardis are living in such a way as to call into question whether or not they possess true, living faith in Christ. Does the *name* Christian genuinely apply to them? The church in Ephesus was in the very same danger."[85]

Finally, the church in Laodicea had become so self-sufficient in its thinking that its members believed they, on their own, possessed everything needed for spiritual vitality and productivity (v. 17*a*). In reality, they actually had become spiritually poor and needy (v. 17*b*). The final result was a complete uselessness for God and his kingdom (vv. 15–16).[86] Once more, a change was demanded for both the church of Sardis and the church of Laodicea.

Notice the progression and connection between some of the churches and their need for course correction. We begin by seeing a church losing a relationship to the Lord yet maintaining its doctrinal purity. Next we see a loss of

---

[84] Patterson, *Revelation*, 121.

[85] Beale, *Book of Revelation*, 273.

[86] Laodicea was known to be rich in every natural resource but water. Cold water for drinking had to be transported from Colossae, and hot water for bathing and medicinal purposes had to be brought in through aqueducts from Hierapolis. The problem on both occasions was, by the time the water reached Laodicea, the cold water was no longer cold, and the hot water was no longer hot. Both had become lukewarm. Cold water is useful. Hot water is useful. However, lukewarm water is not. The only effect it produces is the desire to spit it out of the mouth. Likewise, the Laodiceans, because they were too far from their source, were no longer useful; i.e., neither hot nor cold. They would have understood this metaphor immediately (see discussion in Patterson, *Revelation*, 138–40).

doctrinal purity, then a loss of doctrinal purity leading to loss of purity in living. Then we see an outward appearance not matching an inward reality, perhaps indicating spiritual death and lack of evangelistic zeal. And finally a church is described by its unmerited self-sufficiency, which led to uselessness for the kingdom. Debates regarding the finer details of what was meant by some of these descriptions and thus what specifically the problem was in every instance may rage, but what cannot and should not be missed is that, again, in each case for all five of these churches, a change was needed and change was commanded. In fact, the only two exceptions in the list are the churches of Smyrna and Philadelphia. Even in these instances, they too are surrounded by difficult situations and impending danger. No guarantee was offered that they would not be in need of a correction. "I am coming quickly; hold fast what you have, so that no one will take your crown" (v. 11).

Furthermore, the warning for each church may be constituted in John's words to the Ephesus congregation. It was a promise for the complete removal of the church's lampstand if they failed to change (Revelation 2:5). According to Revelation 1:20, the lampstand is a metaphor for the church itself. Essentially, if these churches did not change, they would lose their name, power, mission, and authority. They would cease to be *the* church. Worth noting may be the observation that many have made before. Where are these seven churches John mentioned in chapters 2 and 3 of his revelation? Perhaps the need for a course correction in the churches we lead today do not rise to this level of seriousness. However, we certainly see here a biblical precedent for change.

One final detail of this passage is significant and applicable for understanding the process of change in biblical leadership. Notice that in addressing each church, Christ addressed "the angel of the church." Perhaps our past assumption without much consideration or knowledge that an alternate plausible view exists is that each church had a specific supernatural being assigned to them. Therefore, it is to this specific "transcendent guardian" Christ addressed and issued the call for each church to "hear." This perspective makes sense and is the one Beale seemed to affirm.[87] This view, however, is one of at least five interpretative possibilities.

> Hemer has indicated at least five reasonably prominent understandings of the meaning of the angel. He speaks of these as (1) heavenly guardians of the church, (2) human representatives of those churches, generally identified as their bishops or pastors, (3) personifications of the churches themselves, (4) literally human messengers who were perhaps the postmen, or (5) usage of the term in "some complex and elusive way or at differing levels" so that no lexical equivalent tells the whole story.[88]

At a more basic level, the possibilities can be simplified even more. Two general possibilities for the lexical range of meaning for the Greek word *angelos* exist: "a human messenger serving as an envoy, *an envoy, one who is sent*" or "a transcendent power who carries out various missions or tasks, *messenger, angel*."[89] Therefore, either the address is referring to transcendent beings or human messengers. If the address is to a human agent, the evidence may be weighted more toward the probability that the angels are indeed pastors. "The above argument does not establish any certainty as to the identification of the angel of each of the congregations

---

[87] Beale, *Book of Revelation*, 273.

[88] Patterson, *Revelation*, 78.

[89] Walter Bauer, *A Greek-English Lexicon of the New Testament and Other Early Christian Literature,* ed. Frederick William Danker, 3rd ed. (Chicago: University of Chicago Press, 2000), 8.

but does constitute the rationale for the hypothesis that the angel may have been the pastor."[90]

The larger context of Revelation 1:9–20 may help bring even more clarity to the use of the designation "to angels of the church." As John's vision on the island of Patmos began, he saw the one speaking standing in the midst of seven golden lampstands and holding seven stars. In the end of the chapter, the Lord explained the metaphor of the lampstand and the stars. Based upon the reference to Daniel 12:3, where the wise are said to shine like the firmament and the righteous are compared to stars, Lenski explained that the designation in this passage to stars should not be understood as the guardian angels of each church. To him, since the word *angelos* essentially means "messenger," both the prophet in Haggai 1:13 and the priests of Malachi 2:7 are rightly referred to as angels of the Lord. His conclusion is significant and helpful for us: "These 'seven stars' are the pastors of the seven churches. They are distinguished for the church as such (lampstands) and yet belong to them and in the seven letters are held responsible for the condition of their churches."[91]

The seven lampstands are the churches themselves, and the seven stars are the angels, or messengers, of the seven churches.

Even though the context of chapter 1 may not bring the level of closure, satisfaction, or finality to identities of the addressees we may desire, whoever the "angels" in the first three chapters of Revelation are, they are never mentioned outside of their association with a specific local church. Patterson, noting that there may be challenges with equating the angels with the pastors and that the evidence is not certain, because of the angels' association with the specific congregation, the position that these messengers were

---

[90] Patterson, *Revelation*, 80.
[91] Lenski, *Interpretation of St. John's Revelation*, 68.

indeed the churches' pastors is the most logical. "The logical expectation of John would have been for the letters to make their way to the one individual in the church who would be most responsible for reading and interpreting the letter to the congregation. How that could have been anyone other than the pastor is difficult to imagine."[92]

Therefore, in the setting of the book of Revelation, that the angels referred to in chapters 2 and 3 are not heavenly supernatural or transcendent beings but pastors may be not only possible but probable.[93]

If those addressed are indeed pastors, not only do we have a biblical precedent for change, but we also can see that the pastor or ministry leader bears the responsibility before God for the course correction. Even if we cannot conclude with certainty that these are the pastors of the churches, we nonetheless see that each church was addressed through a representative. Regardless, the burden and responsibility of the change was placed on some individual by the Lord himself. Furthermore, if a specific person does not take the responsibility to lead the change, then no one is actually accountable for the change. In ministry, the person who must take responsibility is the ministry leader. So how do we take the responsibility for change? How can we lead change in the church or ministry we have been called to lead? Moreover, can we do so and survive?

An Eight-Step Strategy for Facilitating Change in Ministry Leadership

If we believe that our understanding of leadership is distinctively biblical, consistent with God's goals for ministry, and actually helpful for achieving success in leading, then it matters that our philosophy for and process of facilitating

---

[92] Patterson, *Revelation*, 79–80.
[93] See Lenski, 68, and Patterson, 80.

change is consistent with our definition. At a minimum, we must guard against our approach being inconsistent with it. Therefore, the foundations, understandings, philosophy, and ultimately practices of ministry leadership should connect with and grow out of the definition of biblical leadership that we identified in chapter 2: "Biblical leadership includes the process of finding God's goal for a specific group of people, instilling that goal in them, equipping them to grow in Christlikeness and fulfill the goal, and empowering them to serve God's eternal kingdom along with you." If this is a biblical description based on a biblical theology of leadership, then even our practice of leading must match our understanding. In the following text I offer eight practical steps for facilitating change that takes into consideration our approach to biblical leadership.

First, the ministry leader must understand that he or she is the agent of change but cannot be the sole proprietor of change. In order for a change to begin, someone has to take responsibility. If the leader is not the person who takes this role, the probability of the change occurring, occurring effectively, and occurring with lasting results is unlikely. As a ministry leader, you are the one who has to take ownership of the change process. You must do so intentionally and strategically. At the same time, you need others to support your decision and to help create a plan for the change. Your mandate is to recognize changes that need to occur for the good of the ministry's mission and to find a team that will work with you from the beginning of the process. In subsequent steps, we will discuss finding the right people to help you and utilizing them as a part of the change process.

Second, the ministry leader must determine whether the change at hand is necessary to accomplish God's directive for the ministry, the goal that holds an eternal significance. Prioritizing your change strategy to focus on mission-critical items does not mean you will never address secondary issues.

It does, however, offer a spectrum on which to evaluate change needs. As such, prioritizing changes can help you see true priorities versus personal preferences and thus offer a paradigm for areas in which compromise with others is needed and appropriate. Essentially, focusing on the changes that relate only to the eternal significance of the mission helps you to lead with wisdom, especially in the early phases of your ministry. It is likely followers will feel as though everything is changing in the beginning of your leadership, even if you have made a concerted effort to change very little. The fact is with new leadership generally, and leading through change specifically, people need a balance between change and continuity to feel the freedom to follow. Focusing only on what relates to God's goal for the ministry safeguards against changing too many things at once and thus creates a platform for the continuity that people need in order to accept change.

Third, the ministry leader must ask whether the change at hand is necessary *now* to accomplish God's goal for the ministry. Building off the last step, not only do you need to know whether the particular change is germane to the ministry's mission, but you should also consider whether the particular change you are considering is one that needs to happen now. Going through this process will help with several items related to the success of the ministry. For instance, avoiding secondary and tertiary decisions will help balance the change-continuity continuum. As a leader, you should focus only on one major change at a time, especially in the early stages of your ministry. This practice is helpful not only for the people being led but also for the person leading as well. Managing multiple changes at one time requires a higher capacity than what most leaders have, even if they believe otherwise about themselves. Make sure to pick the individual change strategically and intentionally and order the priority of the changes holistically, so as to have the maximum impact and reach the ultimate goal of the mission. Obviously, there are exceptions to this rule, such as items that relate to legality, safety, and biblical fidelity. Therefore, if the change is fundamentally necessary because the good and safety of people are in jeopardy or for the strategic advancement of God's goal for the ministry, take it on. If not, be willing to let it go for now and come back to it later in your leadership planning.

Fourth, the ministry leader must determine the decision-making structure of the ministry, both formal and informal, in order to create a process that will facilitate change successfully. We established at the beginning of this section that a leader cannot drive a change on his or her own. This step will help you determine both how you need to make the change in your particular ministry and who the appropriate parties are to help you accomplish it. Both formal and informal decision-making and leadership structures exist in most ministries. Formally, the church's or ministry's bylaws should direct you to who has both the responsibility and authority to make particular decisions. This authority usually includes some derivate of either a middle-out or top-down process. In other words, the right to and expectations for making decisions and setting vision either exist in committees (middle-out) or it has been formally given to those who hold official positions in the church or ministry, such as a pastor (top-down). Nothing can derail a new ministry, hiring a new staff position, adding to an existing ministry, or implementing a new discipleship and mission strategy faster than failure to follow the appropriate and expected formal policies of the ministry when creating and implementing a change. Even if the majority of followers are in favor of the new direction, this mistake may invalidate the work, which was previously completed up to that point in the process. Furthermore, a loss of any momentum that has been gained may occur because the entire process must be restarted from the beginning.

Often when this happens, the chances that this particular project can be recovered decreases. Therefore, know the formal structure of the ministry and follow it precisely as you begin to think about your strategy for change.

Most ministries have an informal decision-making process as well. This is especially true in smaller ministries or churches but exists on some level in almost every ministry. Usually some person, or in some cases a group of people, has been established as the *de facto* or informal leader of the ministry. Most importantly, the people trust him or her. The net result in most instances is, if he or she speaks in favor of a decision, most people will accept the new direction and follow. Likewise, if he or she speaks against or opposes the change, most people will reject the new strategy and will not follow. Typically, this type of decision-making process is referred to as a bottom-up leadership structure. A leader will do well to find out who this person is, or these people are, and engage and include them early in the discussion about the proposed change for the ministry. This process frustrates many leaders, especially first-time ministers. Regardless, this structure is often the reality for many churches and ministries. You would be wise at least to think through this possibility as you are considering changes and a change strategy for the ministry.

Fifth, the ministry leader must strategize a plan that uses the decision-making structures of the ministry in order to create buy-in from key leaders and generates openness from the congregation. This step is connected closely to and is an outgrowth of the first and fourth steps in this change strategy, and it really has two components. As a ministry leader, you should devise a plan that follows the formal structure and ministry policies precisely, including determining which people and committees must be involved in creating the strategy, funding and staffing the work, communicating the process, and implementing the plan.

What votes or congregational approval are necessary? When should we plan to conduct the required meetings? If your followers hear other trusted voices from within the ministry (i.e., the informal leaders) communicating both the need and plan for the change, then the ability to accomplish the desired outcome with less resistance increases significantly. To neglect either your responsibility to lead the change or the employment of others to support the change increases the difficulty of leading the people. Therefore, learn both the formal and informal process for leading in the ministry, and employ these processes as you do so. Be precise. Agree on who will do what and when it will be done.

Sixth, the ministry leader must communicate the strategy for implementing the change. Not much can be added to this particular step other than to point out that if the leader does not create a detailed and workable strategy (step 5), then communicating the strategy is an impossibility. From personal experience, I have found that people will often oppose a change not because they are against it in principle but because they are confused about the details. Communication can help with this problem. Once you have an agreed-upon strategy in place, communicate to everyone. Begin communication as early in the process as is appropriate. Use as many different means of communication (i.e., announcements, videos, emails, letters, testimonies, social media, newsletters) as possible. If you believe you are communicating an appropriate amount, you probably are undercommunicating from a follower's perspective. If you believe you are overcommunicating, you probably are approaching an effective amount of communication for your followers. By the way, did I mention that you should communicate?

Seventh, the ministry leader then must systematically implement the change. This step is where the rubber meets the road, so to speak. In this step, you, the necessary committees, and the appropriate leaders and individuals will begin the change strategy. Resist the urge to be hasty and begin too soon. Make sure you have indeed dotted all the i's and crossed all the t's before you begin. Check and double-check the entire process with the entire team. If you have the opportunity, have someone from outside the ministry examine your strategy, plan, and goals. This person may have the ability to see something you and your team have missed. Furthermore, be strategic with the when and the how of your implementation. For instance, if you are beginning a new Bible study unit, then a fall start date usually promotes maximum impact and a higher success rate than one in the summer. Go over who will do what, when they will do it, and who is accountable to whom one last time. If you have done your work in steps four, five, and six, step seven becomes a lot easier and smoother. Now you are ready to implement, but as you begin, do so with an eye toward and in expectation of step eight.

Eighth, the ministry leader must understand that change is always an ongoing endeavor; evaluate the strategy, adjust when necessary, and continue the progress. Recognize from the beginning that it is unlikely that any strategy will be perfect the first time out. A better chance exists than not that your plan will require adjustments several times throughout the process. You have to make a decision from the onset of considering the change. Is the goal to protect your ego and get your way? Or is the goal to accomplish the needed change for the purpose of reaching the maximum impact of God's goal for the ministry in the most efficient way possible, even if specifics or details are not what you preferred or suggested? Because of failure to remember the ultimate goal, step eight is often left out of the change strategy and is never a serious consideration for many ministry leaders. As a result, changes have a higher rate of failure than they could have had or, at best, have less of an impact for the ministry's mission than anticipated. The absence of an evaluation plan can hinder greatly the ministry's ability to reach the desired outcome and sabotage the leader's credibility, which is needed to facilitate change in the future. One reason these results often occur in a change strategy with no evaluation process is because, without commitment to evaluate, ministry leaders do not have a way to see needed adjustments and what is preventing progress until the project is already unsalvageable.

Therefore, the evaluation plan should include several details, including determining when and at what intervals progress should be evaluated. I suggest meeting on a regular basis, such as every week or two early in the implementation process. This is one way to minimize the danger of missing necessary adjustments before it is too late. Once you have established a regular routine, the work has begun, and the team sees some level of desired consistency, you may reduce the frequency of your evaluation meetings to once a month. Once the change has become the new norm, you may reduce your frequency of meeting even further to once every six months or even once a year. However, exercise some caution here. Make sure you are indeed at a place in which the team feels safe to reduce to these less frequent meeting intervals. You must also have in place some type of way to measure the process and outcomes. As the old axiom goes, "That which cannot be measured cannot be improved." Agree on how you will evaluate success and know that the change is achieving the desired results. As with everything else, I suggest being as specific as possible here. Finally, hold the process and any personal preferences lightly, but hold the change for the good of the ministry tightly. Remember, the ministry and the ministry's God-given mission is the point.

The process for change is not easy and perhaps not for the faint of heart. Furthermore, this list is not intended to be one-size-fits-all or an exhaustive strategy that can be employed with no consideration of specific contexts. Surely, adjustments will be needed along the way and other details added to lead successfully your particular ministry through any new endeavor. Ultimately, these steps, as with any others, must be joined with and submitted to the wisdom of the particular leader or leaders that God has placed over the specific ministry. Every situation is unique and presents its own set of challenges. However, these steps offer a baseline, or a place to begin, major considerations to be made, and a process with general guidelines for any change. Perhaps, however, more importantly than a set of steps to be followed are two additional factors for a leader who is attempting change to consider. Each of the steps must be yielded to these two principles for succeeding in leading change.[94]

Two Important Factors for Succeeding in Change

First, leadership capital must be earned and in sufficient supply before the ministry leader attempts to lead the ministry through change. Many an attempted change and entire ministries have been shipwrecked because a leader underestimated the importance of earned and recognized trust in implementing new work. Malphurs identified a five-year progression of moving from chaplain to pastor to leader.[95] He described the early part of a minister's leadership as the chaplain stage. In this phase, followers give the

---

[94] Practical examples of the eight-step strategy for leading change in ministry leadership will be used to show how to "add to the work" in chapter 11.

[95] Aubrey Malphurs, *Being Leaders: The Nature of Authentic Christian Leadership* (Grand Rapids: Baker Books, 2003), 52–55. The "Three Pastoral Stages" is one of several factors that Malphurs identified as a component of the context for leadership credibility and the ability to lead others.

leader only basic ministerial authority that relates to public ministry, such as worship, funerals, and cursory visitations. He described the second part of a minister's leadership as the pastor stage. In this phase, followers give the leader a more intimate ministerial authority that relates to private ministry, such as the birth of children, deaths, and weddings. He described the third part of a minister's leadership as the leader stage. In this phase, followers trust the leader enough that the leader has earned the right to give some level of meaningful direction to the ministry.[96] You almost can see these stages as they develop in most ministry contexts.

From personal experience, I believe certain factors may mitigate or speed up the process of gaining the right to lead change. These include such actions as a leader managing a crisis well or a leader's willingness to be accountable for a mistake. Nonetheless, you cannot overestimate how important a leader earning credibility is before he or she attempts to facilitate change. Whether you agree with one specific timeline, the fact remains that stages of gaining a follower's trust are a real factor, and a leader must have sufficient leadership trust built in order to navigate change successfully. The need for leadership capital, then, is imperative in order to implement change in a ministry setting.

Second, a positive rather than negative approach gives the leader a higher chance of gaining follower favorability and successfully completing the change. A leader can approach and discuss the need for a change by talking about the need to fix a problem in the organization. Here the leader discusses moving away from a negative of the past. This obviously is the negative approach. Alternatively, a leader can talk about the untapped potential that lies ahead for the organization. Here the leader discusses moving toward future opportunity. This obviously is the positive approach. As a leader you can

---

[96] Malphurs, 53.

communicate the need for the change in either a positive or negative way. My perspective is if you are going to make the change anyway, why not take the positive approach?

One example of how you may be able to employ this tactic is to build a call to and strategy for change from the positive components of the ministry's DNA recognizable in its history. Begin by finding the successes the ministry has enjoyed in the past, and then lead your followers to recognize and acknowledge those emphases. You may even plan an actual event to celebrate major milestones that highlight the particular component of the DNA you find valuable for the ministry's future. I have heard some leaders sarcastically ask the question, "What if the ministry does not have any discernable strengths in its past?" I believe the attitude behind the question is shortsighted at best and unfair at worst. The truth is there is at least one part of every ministry's past that is good. God has been faithful to and through this ministry or else it would not exist. The leader's job is to open his or her eyes, do the hard work of looking for it, and highlighting it when it is found. Once you have identified the positives and helped your followers celebrate, then invite leaders, committees, and other individuals to help create and implement a strategy that will carry this part of the DNA into the future of the ministry.

A leader can choose either the negative or positive approach to producing change. You can criticize the bad in the ministry's past or you can celebrate the positive in the ministry's history, using positivity as a tool to ask followers to help in re-creating that success in the future. The change strategy for the ministry has a better chance of acceptance if the latter approach is taken. Therefore, I always encourage a leader to choose the positive tactic if possible when communicating the need for and implementing a change.

Case Study

At Third Baptist Church in Somewhere, America, you have hit another snag. Two years into the new ten-year ministry plan focusing on evangelism, missions, and disciple making, you have discovered a glaring oversight and deficiency in the past and present ministry. Especially as it relates to the church's missions commitments, you realize there is a hole in the church's mission work. Historically, Third Baptist's DNA has been mission-oriented and has been known to be very supportive of missions. After some review of past campaigns and promotions, however, the majority of that support has been financial and prayer-focused only. There has been little to no hands-on involvement, commissioning of missionaries from within the congregation, or participation in short-term mission projects. You have noticed that this mindset has carried over and crept into the implementation of the new ministry plan as well. As you see it, nothing has changed functionally. You now believe a course correction is necessary.

As a result, the staff has been praying together and studying to discover the feasibility of the church engaging in a comprehensive mission strategy that includes an international partnership. You have taken the process seriously and have sought the Lord's leadership to discover what size commitment your church can take on. The staff has come to a decision and believes it is time to create a detailed plan including manpower, time period, processes, procedures, and finances. The staff is unified and in complete agreement that this new work is something the church can and should be willing to do. Taking into consideration the eight-step process, write a detailed strategy for how you would lead the church through this change. Be specific, and be sure to include details such as who you would recruit to help, why these individuals and groups are the right people for this process, how they would help, how the need and plan would be communicated to the congregation, the steps you would take to implement the strategy systematically, and how and when you would evaluate the progress. You may supplement your answer with other information and sources, but be sure to include information from our study in chapter 9, especially as it relates to the biblical foundation and mandate for change.

Chapter 10

Assessing the Work

In this chapter, we will explore the concept of assessment and how to evaluate what you are personally and collectively accomplishing. We can get stuck in simply repeating last year's calendar or rebranding a ministry or program without evaluating to see whether it is still achieving the intended goals. Sometimes we are further along than we thought; other times we are unintentionally drifting slightly off course. Have you ever been on a hike at a state or national park where you had a trail map to follow? A trail map allows you to enjoy the nature hike within boundaries to keep you safe. By following the map, you don't drift off course. Assessment allows ministry leaders to look at our ministry trail map, informed through the lens of God's Word, to be sure we have not drifted off course.

A firm foundation in Christ is an essential foundation for ministry assessment. I believe wholeheartedly that all assessment should begin through a season of prayer. We often look to ourselves and other people for assessment when we first spend time with the Father in prayer. Often, ministry leaders receive feedback from volunteers, leaders, or those in the congregation. This type of feedback can be helpful as part of an overall but surface-level assessment of the work. It should always be taken with a grain of salt, so to speak. For example:

> ➢ Courtney is your most involved teenager who always attends every camp, DNow, and mission trip. She is full of life and happy to help. She is also full of ideas and desires to share insight with you and others to improve her youth ministry's overall work.
> ➢ Jason is a pastor who loves ministry, but his many opinions seem limited only to how the ministry could improve.
> ➢ Larry is the parent who is always there and gives relentlessly to serve and has a teenager involved in the church.
> ➢ Marie is a senior adult woman who is a prayer warrior for ministry in the church and is quick to remind people of all the "perceived" problems of anyone attending her church.

You should not consider one person's views to represent the whole unless you have data to confirm those opinions. Regardless of how you choose to receive feedback, it should fit within a larger process for ministry evaluation. Informal, organic feedback can be used each week as an ongoing ministry assessment while a more formal assessment can be used in more structured ways. Wise leaders must learn to weigh the importance of suggestions and comments so the feedback doesn't hinder your important, ongoing work.

Standard metrics for assessments are the ones we can simply count.

> ➢ How many children attended vacation Bible school?
> ➢ Did you notice our worship attendance is increasing?
> ➢ We sure can pack a room when we have these special events. This room holds five hundred people!

Sometimes in ministry, we evaluate the work based on excitement or attendance. Personally, my heart leaps when more people are attending small groups and weekly worship gatherings. I love a unique event that draws many toward our ministry for the first time and introduces them to the life-changing gospel of Christ.

In every church, regardless of size, the greatest need has always been more leaders or volunteers to invest in ministry. Jesus reminded us, "The harvest is plentiful, but the laborers are few" (Matthew 9:37 ESV). Therefore, when we begin to assess the work as we attempt to gather the harvest, we need to remember that those serving are an important consideration. As leaders in the church, we have to assess the ministries and determine whether they are accomplishing their intended purpose, whether they need to be retooled to move forward, or whether they need to be eliminated. Regardless of the results of assessment, be careful to consider the individuals impacted by any decision made.

The first step in assessing the work is to inventory.
An essential aspect of ministry leadership is developing a plan to assess the overall effectiveness of your ministry. The following are examples of excellent inventory questions:

➤ How many people serve in ministry?
➤ What areas need more people in order to reach optimal effectiveness?
➤ How many people are required to effectively facilitate worship services? (This includes platform personnel, worship team members, first impressions, parking lot personnel, and any ministries occurring during the worship service).

Since people only have a set amount of time to give, the inventory process may reveal that your church could be attempting more than you can effectively train, staff, and manage each week. Suppose your significant events are draining focus due to planning, gathering the needed resources, advertising, and executing essential events. In that case, you may need to limit the number of big events or even restructure to focus the attention on the weekly ministries that have a more lasting impact on people's track toward Christlikeness. I have led in both children's and youth ministry and understand the importance of big events. We cannot discount the impact of summer camp, retreats, or other events requiring significant planning and resources. I remember each epic event I attended as a student and planned as a youth pastor. I have notes from sermons from fall retreats, camps, and mission trips as a student. Each of these—events, camps, and weekly schedules—should be evaluated to be sure you are collectively accomplishing the ministry's vision and mission.

Volunteer leaders and their development is key to accomplishing the work in the most effective way possible. Each volunteer should evaluate their involvement as a leader. The overall collective work should also be assessed with a group of people that considers the big picture. List each component of your big events, trips, and weekly planned opportunities. As a ministry leader or volunteer, how much time do you have each week to be an event planner, leader, teacher, or facilitator? Which aspect of serving reenergizes you for ministry? Are you doing things that could be delegated to others? Are you doing something that should be done by someone else? What components of the work can only you do? The key in assessing the work, according to Welch, is assigning work or tasks to individuals.[97] When we decide on an aspect of the work that needs to be completed and grant the job to someone else, we have to equip them and oversee the work to ensure it is accomplished.

---

[97] Robert H. Welch, *Church Administration: Creating Efficiency for Effective Ministry*, 2nd ed. (Nashville: Broadman and Holman, 2005), 26.

Some leaders love events and thrive on executing them well. They awake in the middle of the night with a logo or name for the next epic adventure. Others love pouring into a small group of people and are energized by studying to lead and listening to care for their group. If you talk to leaders, you also learn some are driven from trip, camp, or retreat to the next big event. They think about the most strategic and effective way to execute events to reach more people. All of these are great, but as we build our ministries, we have to consider individual strengths and place our people within teams that allow them to live out in a way that energizes them. If you are an event-only or trip-only leader, then you still need to be a part of regular ministry so that the people will see you as someone they can trust on those occasional excursions.

As you evaluate, seek ways to increase effectiveness rather than focusing on criticism or aspects not working well.
The main thrust is always to reach people with the gospel in a way they will respond to. As they follow after Christ, these disciples should devote their time, talent, and treasure to those things that will grow their relationship with Christ. We cannot control some aspects: schedules, families, community schedules, pandemics, or any of the many other factors beyond our influence. We can influence the culture in these areas, but we cannot control them like a thermostat.

What can we control in our ministry environment? We can impact the ministry culture and provide leadership that moves people to think critically and lead in a way that redeems the time spent participating through our programmed opportunities at church. A challenge to assessing the concepts or approaches to ministry is looking from a historical lens at how far you have come. Don't forget to look ahead to what your church can become.

As you evaluate your ministry, find some people outside your ministry or church who can lean in and give you guidance.

I have always had a few men with whom I build a relationship. We share life and speak truth to one another. A leader needs accountability. We all make mistakes, but we should not have ongoing sin that is not dealt with in our lives. Mistakes are things like, "I ordered too much food," or "I did not plan well for the event," or "In the midst of a busy week I spoke more harshly than I realized." If we are attempting to do too much, then we are less likely to be the person we need to be as a leader. Sin finds ways at every level to challenge the ministry we are trying to achieve. We need people we can be transparent with as we evaluate our journeys. We need to be reminded that any of us are potentially one decision away from wrecking the ministry—this why personal assessment with a few trusted spiritual advisors should be ongoing.

In the ministry space, we also need people to lean in and evaluate where we are compared to where we believe God leads us to be as a ministry. Everyone needs a few close people who can lean into us, and we lean back, so we have a healthy community as leaders. Personal health in ministry is needed, and it is appropriate when looking at the overall health of a ministry that the leader also assess his or her own health. Each of us needs to consider ways to improve our diet and exercise. We also need to think about the health of our relationships and how to improve in this area. And we must guard our minds and revisit where we dwell mentally and what we consume. As ministry leaders, we cannot neglect the commandment to "love the Lord your God with all your heart, with all your soul, with all your mind, and with all your strength" (Mark 12:30 CSB).

The goal is to prayerfully review what is working to achieve ministry vision and mission.
Chances are some good things are happening that need to be celebrated. It is healthy and encouraging to review where you

have come from and forecast where you are going. Although you will be reviewing aspects specific to your ministry, you should also consider what has occurred in the community, among sister churches, within your church, and then your particular ministry. Some factors may have impacted your work that you did not think would.

For example the school system could change its rules and times for after-school practices. This would impact attendance for Wednesday nights and some other crucial areas of ministry. Your assessment needs to consider the whole picture of your work, including factors outside the church. Sometimes we conduct reviews without realizing other churches, ministries, or leaders could be walking a similar journey with a similar trail map with similar challenges. As you conduct your assessment of the work, talk with ministers and leaders in churches with similar community and church factors to see whether the elements are an anomaly or possibly a new state of reality. You have to be careful not to let this mutual assessment drift to comparing with others because they are not the standard. You also have to be sure this is not the only assessment you conduct, and be sure not to stop analysis simply because you find answers that make you comfortable.

Consider the casual assessment as you do the work each week. As you go about your work, seek feedback on aspects of ministry from those you encounter. This can be a great way to receive input from a wide range of people and perspectives. Friends, accountability partners, other ministers, leadership team members, and regular participants can provide insight about your ministry and the overall work you are leading. People will usually give you feedback if you probe them for their thoughts. We all have many opinions about life and feel that our voices matter, so be sure you are ready to receive the feedback you ask for. Be intentional about how you word what you ask concerning seeking feedback.

Remember, don't just change a ministry or strategy based on the complaints of a few people. Assessment should always include others' critiques, but a decision should not be made just to appease a negative voice. Sometimes we let negative feedback unconsciously drive us to become cynical of people, churches, or communities. I recently heard a leader state that sometimes our enemies are the only ones who will be honest with us. When feedback is not what a leader or team desires to hear or deal with, we should consider the source and substance before making overarching changes or decisions. Consider the big picture in your process as you look to individual pieces of the overall work. You may have a great ministry, but one way it could be enhanced is to transition it from functioning as a silo in the church to be integrated within other ministries' framework.

Scripture should undergird any ministry evaluation.
The logo, events, schedule, and curriculum are essential components to the ministry and should be considered as you evaluate. However, the broader consideration should be engaging people with the Bible and connecting them to serving within the church. It is essential to not drift from the biblical standard of the main goals for a local body of believers. You can probably think of a time in your leadership or in another church when the ministry was about a person or significant annual events that everyone talked about. In the beginning, the person or events were not intended to be the focus or driving force. Consider whether you or any aspect of the ministry has drifted from the intended target.

10 Questions for Assessing the Work

1. What is the current mission and philosophy for the church and its ministries, and why?

2. What is the worship attendance snapshot from the last three years? Think about digital online attendance and in-person attendance.

3. What is the annual income for each of the last three years? And how many giving units contributed to that total?

4. What is the current staff structure and total number of employees?

5. How old is the infrastructure, and what are the major cost factors for significant expenses? Consider technology upgrades, mechanical needs, deferred maintenance, and systems that will be big-ticket investments items.

6. How many unique ministries are there? Calculate how many adult volunteers are needed to serve and make those opportunities happen each week, month, and year. Consider as many ministries as you can: small groups, worship teams, age-graded ministries, first impression, special events, etc.

7. What are you doing well in ministry that is reaching and making disciples?

8. Are there any missing components in reaching the people within a five-mile radius of your community?

9. What impression does the community have of your church? If your church were to disappear, would your community notice?

10. What are the changing community or church challenges that should be addressed in the next one, three, and five years?

Leadership is a crucial component of any assessment strategy. Assessing the church areas and the people should not be a draining endeavor but a healthy exercise toward improvement. Tod Bolsinger states, "Leadership is energizing a community of people toward their own transformation in order to accomplish a shared mission in the face of a changing world."[98] Whereas assessment may not be everyone's favorite activity, it can be nurtured by leadership to become a useful endeavor that helps the organization.

The assessment process should strive to look at four Cs within your ministry.
First, your church should be engaged in an ongoing strategy to connect people to a weekly *corporate worship* gathering. Many Christians are changing their mindset toward what a "practicing Christian" is. According to research, if you attend corporate worship once a month, you fit into a practicing Christian category.[99] Second, as you assess your church through the lens of corporate worship, look to the *critical components* of ministry that need to take place to reach and make disciples. Third, I encourage you to assess the *commitment* required by staff and volunteers to make the first two priorities possible. It takes people to accomplish the ministries of the church. As you consider the overall worship gathering and ministries, you can identify where resources are missing or lacking in order to take steps to enhance the overall work. Fourth, you have to evaluate the *cost* of the overall work. Time, talent, and money are all factors that have to be considered. Each ministry component takes time to execute. Each aspect also requires people to invest their talents and gifts, which means stewardship of the priorities

---

[98] Tod Bolsinger, *Canoeing the Mountains: Christian Leadership in Uncharted Territory* (Downers Grove, IL: IVP Books, 2015), 42.
[99] "Five Trends Defining Americans' Relationship to Churches," Barna: State of the Church, February 19, 2020, https://www.barna.com/research/current-perceptions/.

is critical. Everything costs in the end, and sometimes this aspect is more than money.

Structural Assessment

The structural aspects of ministry that always need assessing are the facilities, finances, and staff. A facility ages each day just like our homes, and equipment ages and breaks down and needs to be upgraded or repaired. It is vital to assess the facility and have a master plan for ongoing maintenance. You can use a spreadsheet to show the significant pieces of equipment, repair dates, and anticipated replacement or life expectancy. It can also be helpful to document cosmetic improvements like paint jobs, roof work, and floor upgrades. Assessing facility management annually will help you be prepared for ongoing and surprising maintenance costs. Buildings will age, and the cost can be significant without a plan.

Finances are an area often assessed in determining whether or not funds are available. Several aspects can help you look at the financial health of your organization. You can review the past three years of financial data for income and expenses to help forecast the financial goals for next year. If you received a large gift, then the chances are it will not be repeated. The routine giving assessment allows you to forecast anticipated income and real expenditures in a typical year. A more significant consideration is the congregation's age. As people retire, they sometimes move to be near family or adjust their own financial goals. Changes in your community's job market and the age of your people can shift your church's financial health quickly in just a few years. Assessing your church's financial stability is an important aspect to consider in the overall work of evaluating the ministry.

While facility costs may be high, the largest percentage of a church's costs is in the human resource category. You need to consider all aspects of a staff structure—custodians, administrative support, ministers, etc. Sometimes positions get added with little consideration for the long-range impact on the congregation's budget or needs. Assessing staff is a crucial component in ensuring you are appropriately staffed in the needed areas.

An emerging area that many churches are looking for more expertise in is media and information technology. As churches of all sizes broadcast their services over social media platforms and other internet sources, the need for people to shepherd the media footprint of the church is growing. Many churches desire to restructure their staff but like the people they already have, and retooling the team is a challenging assessment process. Over the last several decades, staff structures have morphed to include individual ministers to preschool children, school-age children, family, and students, which for most of the twentieth century were volunteer positions. Staff structures will always be tweaked to address the current concerns, but ongoing assessment is needed to ensure the design fits the church's needs.

Assessment of the staff structure and needs is different from individual staff evaluation. We need to evaluate our paid staff and our volunteers. A simple job description that outlines the mission and need for their role with a bullet list of their position's responsibilities and expectations is a simple administrative detail that does not take a lot of time to create. When standards are established, it is easier to assess areas of improvement. In business, performance appraisals and performance correcting are standard terms because companies recognize that people are their biggest asset. It is even more so that people are the biggest asset to the church's work, and thus we should value our people enough to provide clear guidelines and an assessment plan to help them be who God has called them to be. Assessment does not have to be considered a negative activity but rather an opportunity to help people grow and develop into who God has called them to be.

Consider these questions as you begin the assessment process to ensure you have the right people and data for a clear picture of your current circumstance:

1. Do I have all the facts and information required to assess the needs of a specific ministry?

2. What information do I need to make wise decisions?

3. Who should be involved in assessing the overall work?

4. Which aspects should be subgroups for assessing the work (i.e., small groups, events, retreats/camps, mission partnerships)?

5. What information do you need to be able to assess your ministries?

6. Who needs to be a part of your process to evaluate the ministries?

7. Do you feel that your current evaluation in place is practical? Discuss with fellow team members how to begin through prayer and deal with intangibles and then move to the tangible aspects of your work.

Chapter 11

Adding to the Work

A leader must act deliberately and carefully regarding change. He or she must balance change with continuity. Furthermore, some changes the leader does not control. The leader rather is a guide and perhaps uses these changes to move the ministry forward. We understand, then, that the leader must at times provide assurance that some things do not change, or at least when they do, that they not occur too hastily. Conflict is another reality in which the leader often will have little to no involvement in creating or controlling its occurrence. There are simply some aspects of ministry that the leader does not initiate; rather he or she is the navigator. An effective leader must be a great manager. However, a time will arise in every leader's ministry in which he or she will be faced with performing that which the title assumes. He or she will have to lead the church or the ministry from out front, directing followers. The leader will have to lead the people to a new destination or to consider a new challenge. You may be tempted to ask at this point, "How important is this component of leadership?" If the ministry you lead is healthy and stable, will that not be sufficient? The truth is without a leader leading, the ministry maintaining its health and viability is unlikely if not improbable.

Perhaps you have heard the saying, "If we keep doing the same thing, we will keep getting the same results." The reality may be even more dire. Instead, if we keep doing the same thing with no regard for the future, we may begin to get *diminishing* results. A failure to recognize the need for new ministries, changes to a structure, or additions to the work can at times cause regression and not simply plateau. I have been blessed in the past to have lead churches that experienced growth. In a couple of instances that vividly come to mind, I did not proactively engage my leadership in discussion about additions related to the growth. We did not think about the need for more space. We did not discuss the addition of small group units. We did not acknowledge the possible need for adjustments of our structure. I did not lead. What were the results? Practically as quickly as the growth occurred, it disappeared. Within six weeks, the ministries looked practically identical to how they looked before the momentum. My inaction may not have caused the ministries significant harm, but it certainly contributed to the lack of forward movement.

As leaders, we want to avoid the same kind of inaction and mistakes. Therefore, we will explore how to know when it is time to add new initiatives or systems to the existing ministries within the context of the local church and parachurch ministries. To begin, we will explore briefly a couple of passages to give us biblical insight into what to expect as we move forward when we add to our existing ministries.

Biblical Foundations for Adding to the Work

There are at least a few instances in scripture in which we see a leader call a church to add to their work. This does not mean that the author's intent was to command other believers to follow suit or to provide a ministry model for first-century churches. The primary teaching point of these passages probably is not an application for when twenty-first-century ministry leaders should add to the work in their ministries. Furthermore, the context between any first-century church and the milieu that a twenty-first-century ministry leader finds himself or herself in has some significant differences. Any reasons for or initiation of additions to a ministry in scripture should not be taken as a one-to-one comparison of the changes we are referring to and considering here. Nonetheless, these examples show that churches in the first century had to add to their existing work as needs arose, circumstances changed, and ministries grew in order to keep moving forward. This gives us a helpful pattern for how to proceed and what to expect. We will explore two such texts here.

First, we'll look at how Paul led one local church to add a missional benevolence ministry for the sake of the poor in another location.

> Now concerning the collection for the saints, as I directed the churches of Galatia, so do you also. On the first day of every week each one of you is to put aside and save, as he may prosper, so that no collections be made when I come. When I arrive, whomever you may approve, I will send them with letters to carry your gift to Jerusalem; and if it is fitting for me to go also, they will go with me. (1 Corinthians 16:1–4)

This passage is not the only place in the New Testament where Paul addressed this request. Portions of the content of 2 Corinthians 8 and 9 seem to address the same collection. Romans 15, which is written after the collection was received on the eve of its delivery, however, may offer the clearest picture regarding the details of Paul's request to the church. From the text, we see that the collection was intended to be a ministry of Gentile believers (v. 27), which was added to the church in order to aid the poor Jewish believers in the Jerusalem church (v. 26).

Therefore, members of a church in one geographical location (Corinth), and specifically those of a different ethnicity, are being asked to contribute monetarily to a church in another geographical location (Jerusalem) that has members who were struggling financially. Certainly the focus of the ministry included both missions and benevolence. Again, however, we must acknowledge that this is different from a five-year mission strategy that a church may implement today to help take the gospel to an unreached people group in, say, India or a three-year commitment to support an indigenous church in a small community in Nicaragua. Nonetheless, Paul clearly led the addition of a ministry in an existing church, and we can learn from his leadership. There are four criteria to meet before adding to the work.

First, a clear need was established (i.e., the poor in Romans 15:26). Second, Paul was thorough in his communication with the church body about the addition of the ministry. For instance, the context of 1 Corinthians 16:1 indicates that this was not the first time the congregation had heard about the collection. And in his second correspondence with the Corinthian believers, Paul once more reminded them of this ministry request. Third, Paul recognized that the church had the financial means necessary to meet the demands of this ministry (i.e., "as he may prosper" in 1 Corinthians 16:2). Finally, Paul included the body in the oversight and selection of the members who would carry out the mission (i.e., "whomever you may approve" in 1 Corinthians 16:3).

The second passage we will consider is Titus 1:5. In this text, Paul reminded a pastor of the need to add more staff to existing churches. "For this reason I left you in Crete, that you would set in order what remains and appoint elders in every city as I directed you." We do not know exactly when the church in Crete was founded or who founded it, nor do we have specifics concerning when Paul and Titus held a joint missionary endeavor on the island. We do know from Luke's account in Acts, however, that the crowd who heard Peter preach the gospel on the day of Pentecost contained Cretans (Acts 2:11). It is possible that some of these individuals were a part of the three thousand who believed that day and at some point after this time carried the gospel back to their homes, thus founding the church in Crete. Furthermore in Acts, Luke reported that Paul harbored on the island on his trip to Rome after his appeal to Caesar (Acts 27:7–12). Was Titus with Paul on this journey? Was this layover enough time for Paul to have a gospel ministry on this island and see the condition of the church? Is this when Paul left Titus with his initial instructions? We simply do not know, and the narrative in Acts does not include these details.

However, what seems clear is the gospel spread through several cities on this island, and people believed. Churches were established but apparently with little formal organization or leadership. At some point, Paul either saw or was made aware of this deficiency. His action of leaving Titus on Crete and his words in Titus 1:5 were his response. Paul, then, clearly was referring to assigning at least one qualified under-shepherd for every expression of the local church in every town. Again, however, contextual differences do exist between that situation and ours. This situation was not necessarily the same as a specific local congregation today adding a new paid associate pastor or a single-staff church deciding to add a part-time youth minister. In fact, there may be a high probability that at least at first these pastors were unpaid elders. Nonetheless, Paul clearly instructed a pastor to add more church leadership. Therefore here, like with the situation in 1 Corinthians 16, we can identify five criteria of the additions and the way they were to be made.

First, a genuine need legitimately existed. Churches needed qualified pastors because they did not have enough of them, but instead these gaps were being filled with false teachings and teachers (v. 10–16.). Second, a specific job description was communicated before the additions were selected. Each pastor was to have the primary job of teaching what was correct and correcting what was in error in the church (v. 9). Third, it appears a formal and careful selection process was expected in filling the openings. Several character qualifications had to be true of each elder who would be appointed (vv. 6–8). Fourth, qualified individuals could be found. A need existed and the church(es) had the means to meet the need. That Titus was supposed to appoint these individuals assumes that qualified individuals existed and could be located. Finally, the leader was charged with taking the responsibility to lead through the process. "To Titus, my true child in a common faith . . . For this reason I left *you* in Crete, that *you* would set in order what remains." (vv. 4–5, emphasis added).

With these two biblical examples firmly established, we will now look at two contemporary scenarios both involving the need to add to the work in ministry. In both of these cases, I will provide a context in which the additions can be understood, give a brief overview of how the process for adding to the work may be considered and applied to this situation, and conclude by offering a feasible outcome.

Scenario #1: Adding Staff to a Church Plant

A single-staff church plant approximately three years old has experienced moderate but sustained growth. After beginning with a core membership group of fifteen adults and a regular Sunday morning attendance of thirty, the church now has a membership of thirty-eight adults and more than fifty people in attendance on a consistent basis on Sunday mornings. The pastor is the only paid staff member. While the extra members and attenders have increased the volume of his weekly duties, he still is able to manage the day-to-day responsibilities. What he is having a hard time keeping up with is the need for certain ministries such as music, youth, and women and men's discipleship. As a result, the two elders in the church approached the pastor and asked him to begin thinking about what paid staff position he would like to add next.

With this context in mind, what types of considerations need to be made in order to add to the work effectively and efficiently in this situation? In order to consider this question, we will briefly go through the eight steps in the change strategy, which were presented in chapter 9, and relate the strategy to this scenario.

First, what considerations are necessary for the ministry leader to be the lead agent of change while not being the sole proprietor of change? This part of the process is unique because in this situation, other leaders in the church have approached the pastor about the need and encouraged him to consider making the addition. As such, the pastor will need to make sure he takes the initiative and responsibility for the possibility, options, and process. As he does so, he should remember and use the two advocates that he already has to not only communicate and implement the addition but also plan the details of the change.

Second, what information is important for the ministry leader to consider in order to determine whether the change is necessary to accomplish God's goal of eternal significance for the ministry? If the goal of the church plant involves evangelism, discipleship, and continued growth, the answer to this question seems obvious. The pastor can only do so much of the ministry himself without both his family and the church family suffering as a result. Furthermore, there are types of ministries, such as music and youth, that the pastor should not necessarily be expected to perform. From the context provided, that the church plant is approaching critical mass appears obvious. This fact does not mean the only answer is to add a new paid staff position or to add it now.

Third, what information is important for the ministry leader to consider in order to determine whether the change is necessary *now* to accomplish God's goal of eternal significance for the ministry? In context, this addition is necessary for the continued success and the eternal significance of the ministry. Therefore, a legitimate need exists. However, that a need exists does not mean that the church must or is ready to meet the need now. An important consideration here that was also present in the two biblical examples is the existence of the means to meet the need. In the case of this church plant, which is still relatively young with a financial situation that has not stabilized, cost to the ministry must be considered. In this case, meeting one need a certain way may cause another problem that impacts the long-term viability of the church or create a barrier to accomplishing God's goal in the present. Therefore, does the church have other options for adding to the ministry without the cost associated with adding another staff member?

Fourth, what considerations does the ministry leader need to make regarding the decision-making structure of the ministry, both formal and informal? In this situation, because of the nature of the ministry and the focus on new growth, the church plant does not have a structure that includes many committees. Formally, the two other elders have been charged by the body in their governing documents to serve as the personnel committee and the finance committee for the time being. The church body gives accountability by officially voting on any major decisions, including items related to finances and personnel. Informally, the two men and their families have been the leading voices among most of the membership, including the new additions. The good news is these men approached the pastor about the need, so they appear to be on board with the needed addition from the onset. In some ways, then, the church is governed both from the bottom up and the inside out. These are the formal and informal elements that must be processed when considering adding to the work in this situation.

Fifth, what information is necessary for the ministry leader to consider while strategizing a plan that uses the decision-making structures of the ministry in order to create buy-in from key leaders and generates openness from the congregation? Due to the way the discussion about adding staff began, creating buy-in both from key leaders and the church body as a whole does not seem to be as much of an issue. Remember, those who are key leaders, both formally and informally so, approached the pastor. They appear to be supportive already, and they are the ones who have the ability to lead the congregation to agree to the decision as well.

Sixth, what considerations are pertinent for the ministry leader to make while planning and communicating the strategy for implementing the change to the church? The primary consideration to make here is when and how the leadership should begin discussing the possible solutions to the need or the potential change to the church body. It is important that the ministry leader does not bring the potential change to the church body too early in the process before the formal leadership has had a chance to analyze the data. A church has a less formal decision-making structure, meaning communicating too early may actually complicate the process because of well-meaning but uninformed people offering opinions. Once the leadership has considered feasible and realistic options and it is time to communicate the change with the entire congregation, it is vital to communicate often. The general rule here is if a leader believes he or she is communicating enough, he or she is undercommunicating. However, if the leader believes he or she is overcommunicating, he or she probably is communicating at the lower end of the effective communication threshold. Since this is a young church plant that only meets collectively one time per week, it should consider using both in-person and electronic communication over a minimum of a two-month time frame before seriously considering formalizing the decision.

Seventh, what information is pertinent and needs to be considered regarding implementing the additions? The big consideration here is the long-term financial burden. At what point could the congregation carry this type of a commitment? Other ways to meet the immediate legitimate need exist. Therefore, considerations should be given to the possibility of hiring interns instead of full-time or even part-time staff, using this opportunity to begin to add more structure to the church with the formation of ministry teams and training and mentoring members for ministry.

Eighth, what consideration does the ministry need to make regarding how and when the evaluation of the addition will be conducted? In whatever solution ultimately is decided to add to the work, evaluation should begin immediately and on a regular basis. More than likely, this will include a weekly evaluation of the solution and added personnel by the pastor, a monthly review by the leadership or personnel team, and a six-month progress report to the entire congregation. In the evaluation, at least three components should be monitored: time management and the completion of new ministry tasks, the progress and growth of the congregation, and the continued financial viability of the church plant.

The most realistic outcome for the ministry context described in Scenario #1 seems to be a short-term solution that would include three components with a goal to implement a more permanent long-term solution in the future. This solution includes hiring interns from one of the local colleges to work with the pastor in the areas of music and youth ministry for $100 per week. Recognizing that the church should have begun already to plan for future growth, the church will begin to correct that oversight by adding more structure to the church with the formation of ministry teams staffed by church members. The church will also implement training events and mentoring relationships for the members in conjunction with the leadership of the church plant's sponsor church. The church will regularly evaluate needs on at least an annual basis with the goal to add additional staff members when the resources become available to do so.

Scenario #2: Adding a Discipleship Unit to a Collegiate Ministry

A collegiate ministry on the campus of a large state school in the Midwest hired a new charismatic and gifted director eighteen months ago. During this time frame, the ministry has experienced 100 percent growth. The new director is strong in the areas of personal relationships, engaging with new people, and public speaking and teaching. He is weaker in the areas of long-term planning, organization, and general administration.

Before this director's arrival, the ministry had struggled over the last decade while having an average of one director every two years. As a result, the ministry never achieved stability. Attendance dwindled during these years, dropping to twenty-five in regular attendance for campus lunches and twelve in average attendance for the Thursday night discipleship classes. Most of the ministry and mission trips were cut during this time due to lack of interest and funding. Now, however, the ministry is seeing an average of nearly fifty people on a regular basis. The biggest challenge with this new growth and attendance is space and effective and continued spiritual growth. Fifty people is the absolute maximum allowable occupancy for the space to which the ministry has access. The director is now faced with the reality of adding more discipleship units or minimizing the reach of the ministry.

With this context in mind, what types of considerations need to be made in order to add to the work effectively and efficiently? In order to consider this question, again we will briefly go through each step in the change strategy, which was presented in chapter 9 and relate the strategy to this scenario.

First, what considerations are necessary in order for the ministry leader to be the lead agent of change while not being the sole proprietor of change? A couple of leading and decision-making processes that are unique to this particular collegiate ministry setting must be considered as the director attempts to lead through this addition. It is evident he is not naturally strong in the area of leadership and organization. In fact, these are two of his most recognizable weaknesses in ministry. Therefore, he will have to make a concerted effort to make sure he is being intentional about planning for the change, leading the progress for the change, and implementing the change. If not it is likely the additions of discipleship units will never materialize or the change will happen but someone else will have to take the primary responsibility. In order to help the director, individuals or leaders from the collegiate ministry's parent organization or board of trustees will have to be consulted and heavily involved from the beginning of the process. The director should also consider key students from within the ministry to help gain interest and openness for these new possibilities among other students.

Second, what information is important for the ministry leader to consider in order to determine whether the change is necessary to accomplish God's goal of eternal significance for the ministry? The considerations needed here seem obvious—reaching new students for Christ and discipling students who come to faith in Christ through the ministry. Therefore, these changes and additions do affect God's goal of eternal significance and the role of this ministry in it.

Third, what information is important for the ministry leader to consider in order to determine whether the change is necessary *now* to accomplish God's goal of eternal significance for the ministry? Not only should the director consider whether change is needed now, but he should also consider whether the ministry has the means of making the additions now. Remember, the ministry had previously been in a decade-long decline, but now weekly the attendance for the one discipleship group consistently is at max capacity. Unless something is done now, the ministry is going to lose its ability to include more students in the discipleship process. Furthermore, with this large number, the ministry already may be less effective than it should be in facilitating spiritual growth and maturity. Since one of the goals of the ministry is discipleship, adding new units is necessary now. However, does this ministry have the resources to add these new units currently? The options the ministry has for making this change now seem to be limited. The ministry either will have to meet on other nights besides Thursdays only, find new locations, train volunteers within the group to lead the additional groups, or create a strategy that includes a combination of all of these components.

Fourth, what considerations does the ministry leader need to make regarding the decision-making structure of the ministry, both formal and informal? More than likely, the ministry has an outside parent organization or a board of trustees that provides oversight and accountability to the director. This board or the chairman should be consulted early in the change process, and any formal decision-making procedure should be followed where applicable. Typically, as long as no budgetary additions are needed and the structure of the organization is not being altered, the board will give the director authority over ministry decisions such as planning mission trips and outreach events and adding new discipleship or ministry groups. However, keeping the board informed on these changes and communicating with them regularly is a good practice.

Fifth, what information is necessary for the ministry leader to consider while strategizing a plan that utilizes the decision-making structures of the ministry in order to create buy-in from key leaders and generates openness from within the ministry? The most significant consideration here is the support and backing of key leaders or respected members from within the ministry. If a culture has been formed already within the large group's Thursday night gathering, splitting the group into smaller units may be met with hesitation or even rejection. However, if trusted voices from within the ministry are in favor of the additions and involved in implementing the change, others in the ministry are more likely to agree to and support joining a new group eventually. This must be considered in the decision-making and planning process.

Sixth, what considerations are pertinent for the ministry leader to make while planning and communicating the strategy for implementing the change to those within the ministry? Much like in the previous scenario, a balance should be found between communicating too much too early and communicating too little too late. Some discussions should be held with leadership, and the feasibility and details of the additions should be considered before communication with the larger group begins. A challenge to communicating with the members of the ministry that a church or church plant will not necessarily face is the school calendar or the semester timeline. Many of the members of the group may not be physically present, and the group more than likely will not meet after a semester ends. These factors must be taken into consideration when planning how and when to communicate with participants. When communication does begin to the group as a whole, corporate discussion rather than formal announcements, social media, and personal contacts from key leadership from within the group must be included in the strategy.

Seventh, what information is pertinent and needs to be considered regarding implementing the additions? The ministry does appear to have the resources to add to the ministry now. However, in order to do so, the director needs more man power. With a group of fifty, breaking the group into smaller discipleship units based on gender and year classifications is one possible approach. For instance, the ministry could split into four discipleship meetings: freshman and sophomore girls, freshman and sophomore guys, junior and senior girls, and junior and senior guys. Regardless of the number of teachers needed for the new groups, the ministry will need to provide access to mentoring for other leaders and at least one other night or location to meet. Furthermore, when to implement the new additions must also be part of the strategy discussion. One possibility would be beginning the planning and communication to the members of the ministry during the spring semester with an aim toward implementing at the beginning of the subsequent fall semester. This approach would allow ample time to create buy-in from the group, provide training and mentoring for the new teachers, and give the director the summer to finalize any details and organize for the launch at the beginning of the fall.

Eighth, what consideration does the ministry need to make regarding how and when the evaluation of the addition will be conducted? In whatever way and whenever the addition to the work is implemented, as with the previous scenario concerning the church plant, evaluation must begin immediately and continue on a regular basis. More than likely, this will include a weekly meeting between the director and the key leaders from within the ministry for the first month. This meeting should include a discussion of adequate space, any concerns or complaints brought up by the participants, and any other potential problems that were not thought of during the initial planning phase. Then, after the first month if the plan seems to be working smoothly, the evaluation meetings should be moved to a monthly review between the director and key leaders. Finally, a semester-by-semester progress report to and evaluation by the ministry's trustees or board should be expected and included in the process. Since the goal of this addition is to increase the ministry's ability to disciple more students effectively, a major part of this evaluation process should include a rubric for measuring whether this outcome is occurring. If at any point this outcome is not being met, adjustments immediately should be considered for the ministry's strategy.

The most feasible outcome for the ministry context described in Scenario #2 includes three or four components. First, the large gathering will be split into four discipleship groups. The building will be divided by temporary wall petitions into smaller meeting spaces. This will allow the freshman and sophomore girls and freshman and sophomore guys to meet on Tuesday nights, while the junior and senior girls and junior and senior guys meet on Thursday nights. Second, the director will initially lead the group of the junior and senior guys while three other leaders from within the ministry will be selected to lead the other groups. As a part of this process, the ministry will provide regular training for the teachers and begin a leadership mentorship program to identify and continuously develop other leaders from within the ministry. Third, these new groups as well as the teacher training and mentoring will launch at the beginning of the subsequent fall semester. This timeline will provide time during the spring and summer to communicate clearly and thoroughly to the group and provide training for the new teachers. Finally, as this plan is implemented, the director and the ministry's board will evaluate ongoing needs and resources on an annual basis with the possibility of purchasing a larger building for the ministry and a desire to add a paid female assistant director who can oversee the women's discipleship strategies within the ministry.

Conclusion

Our goal in this chapter has been to provide examples of how you can avoid inaction when action is needed and thus function at an effective level as a ministry leader, especially as it relates to adding to the work in a way that makes the most kingdom impact. With this in mind, there are two overall practical aspects from this chapter related to knowing when to add to the work. First, when the pain of *not* making the addition for you, the people, and the mission of the ministry is greater than the pain necessary to make the addition, the time to consider the addition is now. By pain, here, we are talking about the price or detriment that not making the addition will cost the ministry related to achieving God's goal of eternal significance for the kingdom. Sometimes you and the people need to experience a legitimate need before you or they are ready to act. Second, as a leader you must both evaluate whether the ministry has the means to add to the work and whether you as the leader have the capacity to lead the addition now. Here we are talking about the resources, both personal and corporate, to address the legitimate need.

When the sum adds up, the time to make the addition is imminent. I hope the leadership components of this book, generally, and this chapter, specifically, help you do so with confidence and competence!

Case Study

Great news! The ten-year ministry plan and missions emphasis is working at Third Baptist Church in Somewhere, America. As a result, your Sunday morning worship attendance has begun to increase. The church is experiencing steady growth and upward trends in tithing and budget projections. The church has baptized several people, including young adults and parents, but this has not caused a noticeable increase in your Bible study attendance. The new families who have joined in this time frame have not been able to break into the inner circle of the church or begun to serve in meaningful ways. No new leaders have emerged as far as you can see. All the people who led Bible study classes, were teaching on Wednesday nights, and volunteering in children's ministries are the ones still serving in these capacities now.

You have noticed over the last six to eighteen months that several new housing units and neighborhoods are being developed within a five-mile radius of the church. You believe that God is presenting your church with even greater opportunities for kingdom growth and impact in the future. The question is how to add to the work in order to both involve new members in leadership and prepare for reaching the new families who will be moving into the community. Write a detailed plan about why and how you will add to the work. Be specific, and be sure to include some support as to why you are planning in the manner you are. Include information regarding legitimate needs, the church's means and resources for addressing these legitimate needs, and your role as a leader for facilitating the process. You may supplement your answer with other information and sources, but be sure to include information from this chapter.

Chapter 12
Administering the Details

In this chapter, we will explore the administrative details of the church organization. Each ministry requires administrative components: human, fiscal, and facilities. This work can be laborious and overwhelming when we would rather be focused on discipleship. Importantly, administrative work supports the overall vision and mission so that the main things, such as evangelism and discipleship, can be accomplished with structure and resources in place.

Most ministers lack joy for administrative details. I get it. Navigating office hours, the weekly staff workflow, and managing access to the building aren't tasks most ministers enjoy. In fact, I'd say most ministers wouldn't list administrative tasks in their top ten on any given week. Yet how do we decide if we have the funds needed to make the requested purchases? How do we navigate cash flow for big expenses and payroll? Administrative details, such as these, can be a balancing act, even causing leaders to lose sleep.

Administration is a biblical gift listed in 1 Corinthians 12:28. "The Greek word for administration is κὔβέρνησις, Dor. -ᾱσις, εως, ἡ, steering, pilotage, Pl.R.488b."[100] Similar to

---

[100] Henry George Liddell et al., *A Greek-English Lexicon* (Oxford: Clarendon Press, 1996), 1004.

the captain of a ship, the general concept of administration is to steer or govern a group of people toward a desired destination. The gift of administration enables Christians to organize, implement, and direct the ministries of the church. While similar to leadership, administration is specifically focused on details and organizing church work. Before you turn the page or move on to a more interesting topic, let's take a look at how administration ensures the work of the church is successful.

Sometimes, administrative challenges can lead to boredom or feelings of being overwhelmed. A simple change in mindset could help you administer well as you consider the overall health of those you lead, church financial stability, and stewarding time and talents to honor the Lord. I (Jody) must confess, the details get me excited and the administrative aspects do not wear me out. I believe they help me minister with excellence. However, I understand that most people in ministry are not excited about these concerns or issues except for their desire that they function well, as to not disrupt their area of ministry. If we can streamline the administrative processes and create a culture of healthy management, then we free up more time to focus on the ministry details that ignite our God-given passion for ministry.

Let me encourage you to approach this chapter with an open mind, asking God to show you some areas where you could tweak to execute the administrative process more effectively. The following short self-assessment is a good place to start.

How Administratively Minded Are You?

Read each item below. Using the provided scale, choose a number that best represents your attitude or feelings toward the work listed.

1—Dislike   2—Neutral   3—Enjoy

_____ Creating schedules for building operations and personnel

_____ Creating and maintaining budgets for ministry

_____ Reviewing contracts for accuracy and details

_____ Updating membership records for accuracy and completion

_____ Evaluating church facilities for risk management purposes

_____ Completing volunteer background checks

_____ Planning the details of ministry events

_____ Aligning ministry programming with overall vision and mission

_____ Auditing financial accounts to ensure excellence in stewardship

_____ Determining volunteer needs for each aspect of church life

TOTAL _____

Add up your total score and write in the blank above.

24–30: You are administratively minded. God has likely gifted you with administrative skills to benefit the local church.

17–23: You are neutral on administrative tasks. While there may be areas in which you excel, it might take a little encouragement to complete others.

16 and under: Administration is not really on your mind. Even though you don't enjoy administrative tasks, pray for wisdom and discernment that you will build your ministry with individuals who can assist you in carrying out administrative tasks.

Now that you know your tendencies toward administration, although through an informal survey, you can move toward integrating healthy administrative practices into your church or ministry. Many leaders simply state that administrative details are not for them. One of the most respected pastors I know told me that we cannot delegate the responsibilities we do not like or simply hope someone else will handle them. We have to know the details of the work—because transitions happen as well as unforeseen circumstances that require the leaders to know the administrative details. You may not have to know *all* the details, but you do need to have an understanding of the process. I've broken these details down into a few short management sections we will focus on:

➤ Approaching the Details
➤ Accomplishing Teamwork
➤ Administering the Details
➤ Managing the Overwhelming Details
➤ Resolving the Details for Success

Approaching the Details

We have to begin the administrative conversation with identifying individual areas of administration. Some details can only be addressed by you, your expertise, or experience, but each team member is responsible for some details in church ministry. If you are married, then maybe you can appreciate my mindset concerning details. When you were first married, did you care about the specific details of how to wash dishes, or did each of you utilize your own method and thus, you were okay with clean dishes? It's amazing that my wife and I have our own process for dish washing, yet we are both satisfied with clean dishes, as long as that is the outcome. During my ministry tenure, I have seen leaders who try to duplicate team members like robots instead of forecasting the work and trusting their team with the intended objectives. God gifts individuals uniquely, and part of administration is empowering personal giftedness in achieving corporate goals.

Each of us can be productive while approaching the details from different perspectives. However, when we deal with time off, budgets, and protocols for ministry execution with facilities, transportation, and the church calendar, then the details should be informed by the organizational policies and procedures. Partner organizations can help churches streamline administrative work, and we are wise to seek their services to complement our personal weaknesses.[101]

I have to admit that I often believe if everyone would use my methods for administration, ministry leadership would be easier and take less time. Maybe you have thought, *If my team leader would leave me alone and just let me work, then I could*

---

[101] For example: Planning Center for coordinating volunteers and ministries; Quickbooks for accounting software; Church Community Builder for events, church membership, and digital check-in; Todoist for organizing your work.

get my work completed. Sound familiar? The perspectives of the individual are numerous, yet if we are doing our work unto the Lord, then our approach to the details matters. We can only redeem the time at hand; we cannot reclaim the time that has been spent. I take my approach to the details each week with the thought of leveraging my life to achieve the best workflow possible in my execution of administrative responsibilities. The challenge may be overcoming a personal bias or preference. In ministry, we should always consider how we can best honor the Lord and be flexible to use those methods that work best, even if they aren't our personal preferences.

Consider the time of day when you are most effective and focused. Use this time to approach the most difficult tasks. An older book on productivity by Brian Tracy uses the term, "Eat the Frog," which means to approach the most difficult and arduous tasks first. Once that task is completed, the rest of your day will feel less stressful.

I focus on email when I am first at the office and right after lunch when I am still getting my mind refocused. After email, I add the key thinking and strategic aspects that need my best clarity of thought and creativity. Then I fill in the tasks that need my attention but are ones that do not require as much from me. After these, I place the items that have to be done regardless of my ability or time. They simply have to be completed. Many books have been written about how to best achieve the details of a job or as a leader to focus your days and time slots.[102] My encouragement to you is find a rhythm to your week and the

---

[102] One suggestion is Matt Perman, *How to Get Unstuck: Breaking Free from Barriers to Your Productivity* (Grand Rapids: Zondervan, 2018). Another suggestion is Clay Scroggins, *How to Lead When You're Not in Charge: Leveraging Influence When You Lack Authority* (Grand Rapids: Zondervan, 2017).

details and continue to refine that rhythm into one you can keep and enjoy as you are doing your work.

A personal framework for administering the work will allow you to have margin with the administrative details. This template provides the leader with a prescribed method of making decisions and dealing with the overall administration to routine or recurring aspects of the work.

We all drop the ball and can miss a detail as we lead. The critical aspect is proving the ability to lead by being sure the details are covered. If you struggle in working through the details, then look for one area in which you can improve. Ministry achievement is reliant on the details being managed so no one gets bogged down in the work. When Jethro leaned into Moses about his leadership in Exodus 18 as it related to the overall administrative details, the process for managing the work in a way that helped everyone was crucial for the people to keeping moving. Don't allow personal mismanagement to get the whole organization off track administratively.

Accomplishing Teamwork

Another consideration is how you execute a strategy for getting your people to work in groups. A team is a great way to come together and work on administering the details together. Everyone has to understand their role on the team and be willing to execute their portion of the details in a timely fashion. You may remember group work when you were in school (eye roll allowed) and the struggle when someone did not pull their weight on achieving the assignment. "The more you can clearly identify who provides actual leadership at your church, the better you can explore what it's truly accomplishing—including questions like whether the group is the best size, uses the best meeting strategies or involves the best people for what you actually need."[103]

A master plan for facilities, short-term goals, and long-range ministry, are important elements for success in teamwork. When everyone understands the organizational vision and mission, the team can pull together to accomplish important tasks, such as the processes for executing the budget, using the facilities for ministry, and recruiting and developing volunteers. In my work as a church consultant, I'm routinely asked for help in these three areas of administration. Regardless of your skill in administration, your church congregation still expects details such as these to be handled with wisdom and care. I've also experienced situations where details caused problems:

> - A Sunday school teacher with their room missing resources
> - The volunteer who did not get reimbursed
> - The senior adult classroom that did not get cleaned after an event
> - A homebound member who was not visited
> - A pastor who forgot about a member who was in the hospital
> - A minister who overlooked the details for an event
> - A worship pastor who did not plan an order of service

A lack of attention to details can quickly derail the most successful and growing ministry.

Another important consideration in administering teamwork is working through age-related and generational differences. Author Haydn Shaw discusses our modern

---

[103] Ryan T. Hartwig and Warren Bird, *Teams That Thrive: Five Disciplines of Collaborative Church Leadership* (Downers Grove, IL: IVP Books, 2015), 28.

workplace that can often employ individuals from up to five generations. Generational differences, such as attention to detail, are important considerations for effective teamwork. Shaw believes "the same generational conflicts that get teams stuck can cause them to stick together."[104] Careful consideration to the varying ages and generations comprising your church staff can really help teams work together for success.

Administering the Details

Each organization has a culture for working through the quagmire of details each week. Sometimes the people that have the most leadership responsibility in an organization do not enjoy the administrative details or navigating them in the day-to-day work. The fast-food conglomerate Chick-fil-A has mastered the team and organization approach that has permeated the corporate business to each individual restaurant. This was an intentional effort by founder Truett Cathy to infuse the organization with a specific culture: so that each aspect was not only excellent, but each customer experienced a top-notch visit. "My pleasure" is the response of all employees throughout the Chick-fil-A organization. The people in the organization have to embrace the concept that everything is for God, which was the driving force for Cathy and his business.[105] The church should have a desire to permeate a culture in such a way that every detail is performed with excellence unto the Lord—whether it is cleaning the facility, answering the phone, managing social

---

[104] Haydn Shaw, *Sticking Points: How to Get 5 Generations Working Together in the 12 Places They Come Apart* (Carol Stream, IL: Tyndale Momentum, 2020), 6.

[105] Steve Robinson, *Covert Cows and Chick-fil-A: How Faith, Cows, and Chicken Built an Iconic Brand* (Nashville: Nelson Books, 2019), 68.

media, leading worship, teaching the Bible, investing in students, or pastoring the flock.

We dedicated a chapter to managing the work, which is closely related to administering the details. If people, calendars, events, finances, and the facility are not managed well, then executing the administrative details will be an ongoing challenge for the organization. People can get overwhelmed in managing the organization because in ministry there is always more work and need than we seem to have time to navigate. The details can be compounded when administration is not a primary gift and can quickly become an area that cripples the work of the local church.

The disciples struggled when Jesus asked them to administer food to the crowd listening to his teaching. This simple challenge required resources for people to gather and distribute food. A financial concern was mentioned in regard to the costs of buying food for so many, and the logistics of the task were overwhelming for some. The circumstances with the two accounts recorded in Matthew have different ministry settings. In the first account, found in Matthew 14, Jesus had withdrawn from the crowds to be alone, and the people pursued him. They were in a more remote setting with limited resources, but Jesus helped them with the details and provided for their needs. In the next account, Matthew 15, we find Jesus having compassion on the crowd because they had been together for several days and everyone needed refreshment. This account reveals a different ministry setting from the first miracle of Jesus feeding the crowds, but both require administrative details. This account required the feeding of several thousand people with limited resources. In ministry we have to be reliant on God's provision while also being able to execute the details to provide for the crowds, smaller groups, and individuals we encounter in our ministry.

Managing the Overwhelming Details

Balancing the people and their stress level, risk of burnout, and overall health can be a challenge when the work begins to pile up. As the organization functions, someone has to be responsible for keeping a pulse on the execution of details, workflow, and timeline for completion while also looking out for the overall health of the team members who are doing the work. As leaders, we can get caught up in our work and forget the key people on whom we rely. Often these are individuals who are always willing to help us in times of feeling overwhelmed or overworked. People need to know they are valued but also that they are more than simply a detail to be handled.

Resolving the Details for Success

Ministry details are important to identify and use to create an overall plan to approach the work with a priority ranking system. I recommend creating a list of ongoing tasks that have to be accomplished each day of the week. Then determine what time of day is best for you to accomplish those tasks. Next, create a priority identification system for ministry achievement. This could be using colored pens, a dry-erase board, Post-it Notes, or whatever you prefer. Place the higher priority items in your best time slots to work through them since you need to do these at your best level possible. Then you can fill the remaining time slots with the rest of the work that is before you in a given day or week.

A basic plan for approaching the administrative details can help you with working alongside your ministry team. In addition, this can improve your own mindset of the administrative work in such a way that the details do not manage you but you work through them in a healthy rhythm. Not everyone gets excited about administration, but everyone can learn to do the required work with excellence. Approaching your work in a mindful, planned-out process will help you experience joy in the details of administrative tasks.

Tips for Healthy Administrative Work

1. Approach the administrative tasks as "unto the Lord," not just as a part of your organization.

2. Find or develop a process for administration that works for you in a healthy way to complete the work the Lord has called you to do each week.

3. Find a process for delegating what you do not do well or do not have the mindset to do well. Remember the unique giftedness of your team members.

4. The list of gifts given by God in 1 Corinthians 12:28 includes administration. Administrative details should not be ignored but rather nurtured as a crucial distinction.

5. Consistently revisit your priority listing for ministry, and be sure the list is up-to-date as you schedule your weekly workflow.

In a fast-paced society that is constantly changing, how far out can we forecast with credibility? We have to be on the lookout for shifts or strategic changes that are needed in order to keep the ministry moving forward. The administrative processes should remain flexible so your organization can adjust to the new realities of remote work, online ministries, and the changing needs of the people. Regardless of culture, climate, or changing needs, administrative skills are important and necessary to the continuance of the local church.

Chapter 13

Navigating Conflict and Difference in Philosophy of Ministry

In Proverbs 27:17, the wise man tells us, "Iron sharpens iron, / So one man sharpens another." Perhaps not intended by this statement is an argument for the existence and value of conflict. Some have attempted to draw this conclusion, citing the fact that iron cannot sharpen iron unless friction occurs. Their contingency, therefore, is if men are going to sharpen one another, friction between them will be present from time to time. This may be playing the metaphor too long and far. However, the sentiment behind the position is true. Whereas in an earlier chapter we affirmed that change is inevitable, conflict is as well. Conflict, and certainly conflict in ministry leadership, is inevitable. And it can be good, healthy, and helpful.

Most of the time when we think of conflict in ministry, our minds wander to the all-too-popular situation in which a church member is mad at the pastor. We have heard horror stories regarding these situations. Ministers have been fired, families have lost primary incomes, and children have been uprooted from their home all because the wrong person or group did not get his, her, or their way or decided that it was time for the pastor to go. Or maybe the pastor did not lose his job, but the church splintered in a very public way. Perhaps you have lived this nightmare. Certainly these situations do occur. These, however, may not be the most common, and are certainly not the only, type of conflict faced by ministry leaders. There is the conflict between a leader and followers. There is the conflict between leader and leader. And there is the conflict between follower and follower. In my experience, the last of these is the most common and often the most challenging to navigate.

My guess is that if you have been in ministry for any length of time, you have faced one or more of these types of conflict. Hopefully the problems and disagreements you have faced have not risen to such a nefarious level in which you, the church, or the gospel was damaged. However, any conflict can become damaging, and thus all conflict must be addressed. Furthermore, since the greatest cause of conflict is people, conflict in ministry will never go away because if people go away, then ministry goes with it. Moreover, the tiniest circumstances can sometimes cause the greatest problems. Therefore, not only is conflict a part of ministry, but navigating and ultimately solving conflict will be a part of your ministry leadership.

In this chapter, we will overview a model for navigating conflict, disagreements, and differences in philosophy of ministry within the local church and other ministry settings. The model is taken from Acts 6:1–7. A reason this passage is helpful in producing a model for ministry leaders navigating conflict is because it is the first recorded occurrence of a disagreement within the church after the ascension of

Christ.[106] Furthermore, the process taken to resolve the conflict is provided in enough detail to be clear in offering several definitive steps to implement for approaching ministry conflict resolution.

Acts 6 as a Guide for Navigating Conflict in Ministry Leadership

The event recorded in Acts 6:1–7 is not the first time the church and its gospel effectiveness had been threatened. Actually, the complaint of the Hellenist widows was the fourth time in six chapters that the church faced opposition or difficulty. This means that the church averaged being attacked nearly every chapter by the time we reach chapter 6 in the narrative. This fact is noteworthy. Furthermore, a couple of patterns imbedded in the attacks seem to have developed and are observable. First, the attack against the church begins from an external threat, such as in Acts 4, and then is followed immediately by an internal threat, such as in Acts 5. Afterwards, the pattern appears to repeat itself with an external conflict followed by an internal one. Second, the disagreement of Acts 6 and its threat to church unity seems to be a direct assault on the influence that was achieved in Acts 5:12–16, namely internal membership purity followed by external gospel proclamation. Often in the early days of the Jerusalem church, then, the saints warded off a frontal

---

[106] Some may argue that Acts 5:1–11, the narrative of Ananias and Sapphira, was the first recorded interchurch conflict. Certainly that situation happened inside the church and held potential consequences for the whole body. However, in context, that event seemed more like the addressing of a public sin and perhaps a case of church discipline rather than a church conflict. The situation seemed to be only between the couple and God, with Peter acting as the spokesperson for the latter. Furthermore, no steps or principles for reconciliation or solving a problem, disagreement, or conflict were given in that case.

attack only to be threatened from within. Acts 6 describes such a situation. The delicate unity of the early church became endangered, threatening the spiritual testimony of thousands of believers. With this context in mind, let us observe three components of the situation in Acts 6 that will be helpful for us to consider as we find a model for navigating conflict in our own ministries.

Notice the Nature of the Conflict Itself

Upon initial observation, the problem appears to be that one group of widows had a need for food and the need was going unmet by the church, especially the leaders. "Now at this time while the disciples were increasing in number, a complaint arose on the part of the Hellenistic Jews against the native Hebrews, because their widows were being overlooked in the daily serving of food" (Acts 6:1). A more literal reading of the text may be, "A grumbling of the Hellenists arose toward the Hebrews." We see this is the clear beginning of a schism between two identifiable groups within the church. "We are only getting one loaf of bread when they get two." Who were the Hellenists? Against a popular and misinformed position, they were not Gentile members of the church.[107] They were foreign-born Jews who had presumably either journeyed to Jerusalem because of Passover and stayed because of the events of Acts 2 or relocated and taken up permanent residence in the city. "The Hellenists ('Grecian Jews,' NIV) were more than likely Jews who had come from Jewish dispersion and settled in Jerusalem. Their language and probably many of their ways were Greek."[108] That some

---

[107] R. C. H. Lenski, *The Interpretation of the Acts of the Apostles* (Minneapolis: Augsburg, 1961), 240.

[108] John B. Polhill, *Acts*, The New American Commentary, vol. 26 (Nashville: Broadman Press, 1992), 179.

native-born Jews did not think too highly of this group appears likely. This particular perspective was represented in the Pharisees who referred to the Hellenists as "second class Israelites."[109] Unfortunately, this mentality seems to be perpetuated, or at least perceived, even in the church.

Interestingly, Luke offers no commentary on the extent or the validity of the complaint. We may be tempted to want more detail than I provided or to ask why. We cannot be certain why Luke does not provide more, but we can draw clear conclusions from the narrative. Regardless of the validity of complaint, the situation did cause disunity, so the extent of the neglect was immaterial. Furthermore, the demands and dangers of the conflict raised an even greater dilemma for the apostles. It was now a gospel issue. Therefore, the conflict was certainly a part of the cause, but it was not the decisive problem. "So the twelve summoned the congregation of the disciples and said, 'It is not desirable for us to neglect the word of God in order to serve tables'" (v. 2). Ultimately, we should recognize the greatest problem is a threat to the teaching and preaching of the Word. "Most importantly, however, the present context suggests that, if decisive action had not been taken to deal with the social issue disturbing the church, 'growth' of the word may not have continued."[110] What we see, then, is that the tearing away of gospel purity led to the endangerment of gospel proclamation.

Church unity was endangered (v. 1), and gospel industry was endangered (v. 2). Disunity in the church always threatens the work of the gospel. It endangers the validity of the gospel through our testimony as a church (although not explicitly

[109] Richard N. Longenecker, *The Acts of the Apostles,* The Expositor's Bible Commentary, vol. 9, ed. Frank E. Gaebelein (Grand Rapids: Zondervan, 1981), 329.

[110] David G. Peterson, *The Acts of the Apostles*, The Pillar New Testament Commentary (Grand Rapids: William B. Eerdmans; Nottingham, England: Apollos, 2009), 229.

in this text, see Acts 5:1–16). If the gospel is not protected effectively internally, the external proclamation of the gospel will affect negatively. Disunity also directly affects the gospel internally (5:12b) by taking time and energy away from the work of the gospel (v. 2). The apostles (the church leadership) not only had the potential needs of widows to manage, which is a substantial need in its own right, but they also had to protect the mandate of the Great Commission. Murmurings, grumblings, and complaints always threaten the effectiveness of the gospel in and through a church. Therefore, if everything we have said up to this point is accurate, the conflict in Acts 6 was essentially an attack specifically on God's goal for the church.[111]

Examine How the Leadership Responded to the Conflict

There is an ongoing debate concerning this passage both among scholars and in the church—does this passage refer to the beginning of the role and ministry of deacons in the church? The most compelling evidence to the contrary comes down to the term used for the office of deacon (*diakonos*) and the fact that it is never used in this passage. "The Seven (cf. 21:8) are set apart for a ministry of 'serving tables', but they are not called 'deacons' and Luke's intention cannot simply have been to describe how the order of deacons originated (cf. 1 Tim. 3:8–13)."[112] As strong as this evidence may be, however, the final conclusion should be withheld and considered in light of at least three mitigating factors.

---

[111] See chapter 6, "Defining Biblical Standards for Leading People," for a fuller discussion of how the conflict in Acts 6 was actually an attack on God's goal for his church.

[112] Peterson, *Acts of the Apostles*, 228.

First, cognates of the word used for the office of deacon are used three times in this passage, two of the times referring to the function that was to be performed by these men (vv. 1 and 2). Second, the first time the office of deacon is mentioned formally in the Bible (1 Timothy 3:8–13), the existence of the office seems assumed, known, and recognized. The background and specific details of the office, such as function and purpose, do not have to be explained. Acts 6 seems to be the most logical origin of the role because no other place in the New Testament approaches such a description. "Although the verb 'serve' comes from the same root as the noun which is rendered into English as 'deacon', it is noteworthy that Luke does not refer to the Seven as deacons; their task had no formal name."[113] Therefore, if it is not here where it began, then where did it occur? Finally, the qualifications and descriptions of the process listed in Acts 6, though brief, seems quite specific and formal. It would seem odd then if what is being referred to here is not an official, or at least important, role. "Therefore, brethren, select from among you seven men of good reputation, full of the Spirit and of wisdom, whom we may put in charge of this task" (v. 3).

Regardless, the context of the Acts 6 passage seems to be the genesis of what later became the deacon ministry of the church and included a formal process for addressing a threat that contains clear principles for addressing conflict. If these men were not deacons, then they certainly seem to be assigned the task of "deaconing." Furthermore, they were appointed as leaders who had the primary task of aiding in the resolution of the conflict. "Dissension among the believers is resolved by the appointment of a new group of *leaders* to meet the particular needs of 'Hellenists' in the community" (emphasis

---

[113] I. Howard Marshall, *Acts: An Introduction and Commentary*, vol. 5 of Tyndale New Testament Commentaries (Downers Grove, IL: IVP Academic, 1980), 135.

added).[114] With this in mind, we can discern a plan of action that is given and implemented to address the situation.

Let us begin by looking at the servants' qualifications (v. 3). There are at least four characteristics that had to be true of these men for them to be selected to lead in this task. The first two are important but straightforward. Holistically, the passage suggests that these men had to be professing believers, but more specifically "from among you" indicates that they had to be members of the Jerusalem church. No outsiders where selected. "Good reputation" indicates that they had to be well respected in and trusted by this congregation. The word literally means "bearing testimony or witnessing." The idea being portrayed may be that each man's testimony must match his life. The final two characteristics are not more significant than the first two, but they may be more directly applicable to the specific situation. These men had to be "full of the Spirit and of wisdom." Perhaps the idea is that they had to be more than ones who simply professed to know Christ, but these men had shown that they are daily led by him ("full of Spirit"). Furthermore, they had to be those who are able to apply biblical truth and theology to real life situations ("full of . . . wisdom"). After all, would this not be their primary task as they served the Hellenist widows and brought them back into the fold?

Also, notice there are actually two sets of servants leading in order to resolve the threat in the church's ministry and mission (v. 4). Actually, the word that the apostles used to describe the focus of their own activity in verse 4 (*diakonia*) means "service" or "ministry" and is the same word they used to describe the focus of the seven's ministry in verses 1 and 2. In verse 2, the focus is on the service of the tables, and in verse 4, it is on the service of the Word. The apostles were not

---

[114] Peterson, *Acts of the Apostles*, 228.

rejecting a responsibility to serve. Rather, the question was a matter of the focus of their service.

> They responded to the criticism which was ultimately directed against themselves by recognizing that the combined task of teaching and poor relief was too great for them. In fact they were able to fulfil neither part of it properly. Their care of the poor had come under criticism, and they themselves felt that they were not devoting proper attention to their prayer and their service of the Word. It is not necessarily suggested that *serving tables* is on a lower level than prayer and teaching; the point is rather that the task to which the Twelve had been specifically called was one of witness and evangelism.[115]

Ultimately, we see two sets of deacons, offices, or leaders are employed to address the problem and maintain ministry focus.

Furthermore, the men they chose, or at least their backgrounds, are significant (v. 5). Take note that all seven men have Greek names. All of them, with the exception of Nicolas, who Luke identifies as a proselyte, were of the Hellenists. "The seven names are all Greek, which suggests that their bearers were not Palestinian Jews; it is true that Greek names were used by Palestinian Jews (Andrew, Philip), but, apart from Philip, these are unlikely names for Palestinians."[116] Significantly, the entire church chose and agreed to these men! Why are these details important? Perhaps part of their rationale for selecting men with this background was one of relationship. Perhaps these particular widows would relate better to these men, and these men would be more apt to give greater care and concern to the

---

[115] Marshall, *Acts*, 134.
[116] Marshall, 135.

widows who came from similar life situations. However, when you consider that these men appear now to be in charge of caring for all the widows, both the Hebrews and the Hellenists, a different picture seems to emerge. Even this act of choosing Hellenists as a new group of leaders in the church was a part of the process of dispelling favoritism, restoring church unity, and addressing the schism that had formed between the two groups.

What should we make of the congregation's involvement itself (v. 6)? The leaders (the apostles) certainly did what leaders do through the entire process. They led. This cannot be missed. However, the church's involvement throughout the entire process, from beginning to end, should not be ignored (vv. 3, 5, and 6). "The solution proposed by the apostles was pleasing to the whole group, which made its selection. It is important to note that the congregation made the selection. The apostles assumed the leadership in making the proposal, but they left final approval of the plan and selection of the seven to congregational decision."[117] We may wonder why the apostles installed these leaders by laying on hands after the church selected them. The ceremony appears much less about the apostles taking over and more about them formally handing over certain responsibilities. "The apostles confirmed the congregational decision by laying their hands on them. . . . In the Old Testament the laying on of hands deals with the transfer of some personal characteristic or responsibility from one person to another, as from Moses to Joshua (Numbers 27:16–23)."[118] This action could be viewed as sanctioning the congregation's decision, but more than likely, they laid on hands to affirm what the body had decided. Regardless, the apostles did not usurp authority but

---

[117] Polhill, *Acts*, 181.
[118] Polhill, 182.

agreed to submit to what the church had decided and thus formally handed over this task.[119]

The leadership and the church body responded in such a way that they ultimately were not deterred from the main thing and thus the work of the gospel would suffer no longer. They led through the conflict the "right" way. As a result, they preserved the servants for the Word and thus the service of the Word (vv. 3–6). The ministry leaders implemented the resolution with an eye toward accomplishing God's goal of eternal significance for the church. This leads to the final component of the situation in Jerusalem that will help us develop a model for navigating conflict in our own ministries.

Take Note of the Outcome of the Resolved Conflict

Luke initially described the result in terms of the growth or increase of the Word. As mentioned, we see the continued spread of the Word (v. 7). Scholars have noted that this phrase may refer to an increase in both frequency and location.[120] We should not be surprised nor should it escape our notice that the very practice, which was under the greatest threat by the conflict, is the ministry that experienced the greatest success as a result of the conflict's resolution. The preaching and teaching of the Word after all was part of what grabbed the leadership's attention in the first place and what they desired to protect when the complaint first arose.

As the Word continued to spread, the number of disciples multiplied, and a large number of priests became obedient to the faith. At any given time, there may have been as many as

---

[119] Polhill.

[120] See Lenski, *Interpretation of the Acts of the Apostles*, 248, Peterson, *Acts of the Apostles*, 235–36, and Polhill, *Acts*, 183.

eight thousand priests attending to the service of the Temple.[121] What certainly is known up to this point in the narrative of Acts is that many of the church's opponents had come from their ranks. According to this verse, however, a great company of them trusted Jesus as Savior. Furthermore, this growth seems to have been ongoing.[122] All of this is significant.

> The passage begins and ends with a record of the remarkable growth in the number of believers in Jerusalem, and the point is clearly made that this happened because the ministry of the word continued unhindered (cf. 5:42; 6:7). This is a critical paragraph for Luke's development of a theology of 'the word of God' (cf. 6:2, 4, 7). At three points in the narrative, he writes about the word of God growing and multiplying (6:7; 12:24; 19:20). Each reference climaxes a section recording the resolution of some conflict or the cessation of opposition and persecution. The gospel is shown to prosper in spite of, and even because of, struggle and suffering. Most importantly, however, the present context suggests that, if decisive action had not been taken to deal with the social issue disturbing the church, "growth" of the word may not have continued.[123]

A Seven-Step Model for Navigating Conflict in Ministry Leadership

With a better understanding of what occurred in Acts, how the leadership and church responded, why they did so, and

---

[121] See Polhill, *Acts*, 183, and Warren W. Wiersbe, *The Bible Exposition Commentary: An Exposition of the New Testament Comprising the Entire "BE" Series*, vol. 1 (Wheaton: Victor Books, 1995), 430.

[122] In the Greek text, all the verbs—"increase," "multiply," and "obey"—are in the imperfect tense, which may indicate progressive action rather a one-time or completed event.

[123] Peterson, *Acts of the Apostles*, 229.

the subsequent results, we are now ready to consider a model for navigating conflict in ministry leadership. As we do, much like with our process for change in chapter 9, our goal is not simply general leadership practices that achieve the "best" results. Once more, we are interested in ministry leadership here. Thus, we aim for our foundations, understandings, philosophy, and ultimately practices to connect with and grow out of biblical leadership: "Biblical leadership includes the process of finding God's goal for a specific group of people, instilling that goal in them, equipping them to grow in Christlikeness and fulfill the goal, and empowering them to serve God's eternal kingdom along with you." If this is a biblical description based on a biblical theology of leadership, then even our practice of resolving conflict in our leadership must be consistent with this understanding. Following I offer seven practical principles that are consistent with and take into consideration our biblical definition of leadership.[124]

First, the ministry leader has to determine whether there is a conflict present that may hinder accomplishing God's goal of eternal significance for the church or ministry. Certainly, any conflict has the potential to become a problem, and a major problem at that, one that hinders gospel progress for the church or ministry. Yet not all disagreements or apparent complaints rise to the same level. Leaders must be willing

---

[124] This model is not intended to be a chronological or exhaustive step-by-step process for resolving ministry conflict. Rather, it includes principles that should guide a ministry leader as he or she works to resolve disagreements and differences over ministry philosophy. Certainly, there are more details and specifics that will have to be included in creating and implementing steps for resolving an actual conflict. Any specific resolution plan must be based on the particular context and details of the situation. Not all conflicts are the same. Therefore no plan or solutions for resolving conflict will be the same. However, I believe these principles are biblical and can guide the leader in a general way as he or she navigates conflict successfully. They are practical principles intended to inform, aid, and offer great reminders in any disagreement.

to employ evaluation methodology and sometimes seek wise counsel to understand the difference. This is not to say that a leader should ever ignore, dismiss, or fail to pray about all concerns in the ministry setting, but he or she must have the patience to refrain from making a mountain out of a mole hill. I recall instances in which I have immediately jumped to action or had a quick emotional response to an incorrect perception. At times I actually created a conflict or schism where there would not have been one. Someone was simply sending an innocent email, or someone was attempting to be heard. Not every perceived issue is "a hill on which to die." Wisdom is needed to know the difference.

Second, the ministry leader must define the conflict or difference as precisely as possible. Let's look again at the Jerusalem church in Acts 6. Luke did not give us an opinion or evaluation of the extent or validity of the Hellenist widows' complaint. Neither does it appear that church leadership, the apostles, spent a great amount of time seeing whether this group was embellishing their accusation. Why? There may be several answers to this question, but I am convinced that the situation had reached a point where it did not matter. The complaint had reached critical mass. The conflict was severe enough that it was circulating, known, and creating disunity. Regardless of any detail, a real problem now existed within the congregation, even if based solely on perception, and the problem had the potential to cause even greater and "eternal" damage. The ministry leaders had the foresight to understand who was being neglected, what needed to occur to address the situation, and where the ultimate threat lay if they did not act prudently. They knew the conflict needed to be addressed and their gospel ministry needed to be protected. They defined the problem correctly and specifically. Ministry leaders today need to develop this skill. This practice will help determine whether a response is necessary, what type of response is required, who should be involved, and the level of involvement you need to give to the situation as a leader.

Third, the ministry leader should involve others in the strategy for resolving the conflict. I must admit that I hate putting out fires, but I really hate putting out fires that I did not start. Even as I write this, however, I know this is one of the costs of leadership, and there is no way to avoid this nuisance if you are going to lead. So count the cost and expect to put out other people's fires. When a conflict arises, you as the ministry leader must take responsibility and ownership. If you do not, no one will. Yet this axiom must be balanced with another truth: you cannot and should not attempt to handle conflict resolution on your own. While you must take ownership, you must also include others. Trust me; you do not have the bandwidth to handle every aspect of every conflict or complaint in ministry by yourself. If you attempt to do so, some other area of your responsibility, probably your primary leadership, will suffer.

Including others also carries a positive aspect. If your goal is solving the problem for the genuine good of the church and not simply "winning" or getting your way, then you must include others. Doing so is invaluable and indispensable to the process of conflict resolution. You should strive to include others who have different perspectives from your own, who have different backgrounds from you, who may disagree with you, who are a part of a group that has a disagreement with you, and who may not even personally like you. Is this not precisely what the apostles and ultimately the congregation of the Jerusalem church did? There is much wisdom in listening to others, especially those who disagree with you. You cannot "see" everything. Others can help uncover details you may miss. There is also much integrity in this strategy because it protects us from our own hearts and fleshly desires at times and may be the most effective way to dispel favoritism and create actual church unity. Many ministry leaders completely miss the value of listening to others because they are afraid doing so may cause them to lose power or control. This is unfortunate because it often sabotages their leadership, conflict resolution, and the effectiveness of the ministry in the end.

Fourth, the ministry leader must include the "right" others in the resolution of the conflict. Not everyone, even good people, have the correct disposition to be helpful in resolving ministry conflicts or disagreements in ministry philosophy. Simply because someone was useful in the resolution of a conflict does not mean that he or she will be helpful in the resolution of every conflict. This does not mean that some who are not necessarily beneficial in a conflict resolution role are bad people, troublemakers, unregenerate church members, or not gifted to serve in other ways in ministry. Myriad reasons may exist for this that are related to nothing more than personality or an emotional closeness to a particular situation. Not every conflict or disagreement is created equal, so not everyone is equally helpful in every situation. Remember, the leadership of the Jerusalem church was selective as well in whom they involved in their conflict resolution: "Therefore, brethren, select from among you seven men of good reputation" (Acts 6:3). Ministry leaders must employ the same wisdom today. Unfortunately, this type of wisdom and recognition happens slowly over time, not quickly—think slow cooker not microwave.

One caveat to this step is that, if possible, a ministry leader should consider and use the two offices in the church— pastor and deacons—when addressing conflicts and ministry disagreements. If this passage is the genesis of what became the role of deacon in the church, then perhaps we can say that the primary function of the office of deacon is "serving and protecting church unity" and the primary function of the office of pastor is "serving and proclaiming God's Word and praying."[125] Therefore, when a strategy for addressing conflict prioritizes the complementary nature of the two offices God has ordained and allows men holding these roles to function in the way God has called them, the chances that the conflict is resolved, overall ministry health is promoted, and the focus on the gospel continues increase dramatically. Since the two offices of the church exist to serve the body, when they are viewed properly and functional biblically, they are often used to mediate conflict in the church.

Fifth, in conflict resolution, ministry leaders must understand the need to consider the entire church or ministry group. This practice does not mean that we air all "the dirty laundry" or make a private matter public unnecessarily. However, two important perspectives must be considered. First, even though we may not give details or make a private matter public when it is not warranted, ministry leaders must not hide, cover up, or lie to others or the entire group in the name of protecting the ministry. It is better to say, "I'm sorry, but I cannot talk about that," than to say, "No, nothing is wrong," when something clearly is. If or when the time does come to address the entire group, we should be as forthcoming as possible with appropriate information. Sometimes a leader can present a picture that he or she knows is not true even if he or she technically does not lie. We must work to avoid this practice. We must not mislead intentionally and unintentionally. Second, if actions and strategies, which are put in place to solve the problem, require formal decisions, the commissioning of new positions, the change of roles, or an addition of a new policy or a revision of an old one, bylaws must be followed and the appropriate people and groups must be included in the decisions. The

---

[125] Waylan Owens, former professor of pastoral ministries, Southwestern Baptist Theological Seminary, Fort Worth, Texas, conversation with the author (January 2009).

Jerusalem church leaders followed this practice in Acts 6. "To solve the problem, the Twelve gathered all the disciples together. Even though the Hellenists had the main grievance, the problem involved the entire congregation; and the apostles wanted total participation in its resolution."[126] By not engaging the right policies and the right people, you may create another conflict, one that is much worse than the original disagreement you were attempting to solve.

Sixth, the ministry leader creates and implements a strategy for conflict resolution in concert with others and with an eye toward accomplishing God's goal of eternal significance for the ministry. The narrative of Acts 6 and the apostles' perspective in Acts 2 informs and helps us immensely here. Remember, the context of the passage was that the church was experiencing unmatched gospel success and impact (Acts 6:1). Because of this, the apostles knew that the strategy for addressing the disagreement had to involve more than meeting a group's need or making them happy at all costs. The strategy had to include the continuation of the church's mission and God's stated goal for the ministry: "It is not desirable for us to neglect the word of God in order to serve tables. . . . But we will devote ourselves to prayer and to the ministry of the word" (Acts 6:2, 4). As a result, they not only maintained their focus but actually increased their impact. Part of this process for us may mean we as the ministry leader have to change, hand over certain responsibilities that we enjoy, trust other people, and follow the congregation's or group's directives when they make a decision. The goal is to make sure whatever strategy is decided on and implemented, the resolution encourages and perhaps even increases the continued accomplishment of God's goal for the ministry. Communicate this to your followers.

---

[126] Polhill, *Acts*, 180.

Seventh, and finally, the ministry leader evaluates the success of the implementation of the strategy for conflict resolution and course corrects the strategy where necessary. This step is very similar to the final step of facilitating change from chapter 9 in that it is unlikely for any strategy to be perfect the first time out. A better chance exists than not that your plan will require adjustments several times throughout the process. From the beginning, plan to meet again, be willing to change the strategy, and expect adjustments. Consider these two components in your evaluation. First, from the outset schedule an evaluation and review meeting. I would suggest doing so one month from the time the strategy is implemented. Include all appropriate parties. Give freedom to speak openly in the room. Allow for the communication of frustrations and perhaps even hurts without getting defensive. Correct any holes in the strategy. Celebrate any victories. And plan to meet again soon. Second, personally evaluate the strategy to make sure the implementation actually allows for the continued accomplishment of God's goal for the ministry. Develop a way or a rubric for evaluating this part of the process and your personal ministry focus during and after the conflict. Remember the goal is to make sure that whatever strategy is decided on and implemented, the resolution encourages and perhaps even increases the continued accomplishment of God's goal for the ministry: "The word of God kept on spreading; and the number of disciples continued to increase greatly" (Acts 6:7).

The Case for Collaborative Problem-Solving in Conflict Resolution

I personally have found that walking through these steps is much more impactful when all parties involved do so from a collaborative problem-solving approach. Collaborative problem solving is essentially the philosophy of problem solving in which all parties involved commit to view the other parties not as enemies to be defeated but teammates to work with in order to resolve the conflict. The issue or situation becomes the focus rather than the other person. Call me the eternal optimist, but I genuinely believe that no conflict or disagreement exists that adults who follow Christ cannot work through if they are willing to approach others collaboratively and with deference. We must be aware of and adjust in two potential trouble areas if we are to succeed in this collaborative approach.

First, we have to manage our emotions. Our emotions are not bad or inherently negative. God made them and created us with them. They can serve us well, are needed, and can be of great benefit. Emotions are a part of what it means to be human. However, sometimes when we are too emotionally close to a situation, our ability to have productive conversations and interactions are hindered. If we are going to implement collaborative problem solving, all parties involved need to understand the impact of emotions to our interactions. To be productive then, sometimes we may have to pray together, suspend a meeting, and reconvene at a later date to allow emotions to cool. Be willing to consider and even suggest this option if you see the need and value of doing so. Second, we have to check our perspectives. Sometimes our perspectives are based on reality, and sometimes they are not. When they are not connected to reality, they can be unhelpful or even harmful to problem solving in varying degrees. Often in our attempt to work through our differences, being too caught up in our own perspective, which may not be reality, results in our unwillingness to listen and inability to hear others. When one person operates this way, the possibility of resolving a conflict successfully is hindered. When more than one person takes this approach, conflict resolution becomes practically impossible. In collaborative problem solving, be aware of this danger. Do not assume the worst motives in other people. Hear the facts. Then attempt to define the problem and understand the details as accurately as possible.

Yield your strategy and perspective of conflict navigation to this philosophy and remember who the enemy is. "Finally, be strong in the Lord and in the strength of His might. Put on the full armor of God, so that you will be able to stand firm against the schemes of the devil. For our struggle is not against flesh and blood, but against the rulers, against the powers, against the world forces of this darkness, against the spiritual forces of wickedness in the heavenly places" (Ephesians 6:10–12).

Case Study

Back to Third Baptist Church in Somewhere, America. As a result of learning the church's past mindset and approach of little to no hands-on mission involvement has crept in and carried over to the implementation of the new ten-year ministry plan, you now are well into the course correction. The staff has prayed together, studied the feasibility of the church engaging in a comprehensive mission strategy that includes an international partnership and has sought the Lord's leadership to discover what size commitment your church can take on. The staff is unified and has come to a decision and believes it is time for a detailed plan, including man power, time period, processes, procedures, and finances.

You have now worked through and written the process for leading the change. The staff has considering the inclusion of all the appropriate parties and church bylaws and begun the implementation process for this type of change. You have come to the time when it is appropriate and necessary to share the vision and plans with the lay leadership of the church for their thoughts, questions, and approval before taking it before the entire congregation. The first meeting is with the deacons. The plan is to present the strategy to the deacon body for input and support. During this first meeting, however, two of the leading men in the room adamantly oppose and speak against the proposal. You are aware of what this means. They, and thus the entire deacon body, now will not approve or back the mission strategy. In the scenario, the likelihood of it going forward with the larger church body is improbable. What do you do?

Taking into consideration the seven-part model presented in this chapter for navigating conflict, write a detailed strategy for how you would lead the church and the deacons through this situation. How would you resolve this disagreement over ministry philosophy with these men? Be specific, and be sure to include details such as defining the problem, who you will involve in the conflict resolution strategy, why these are the right people for this process, how and when the church will be involved, what you will do to make sure the strategy brings resolution with an eye toward accomplishing God's goal of eternal significance for the church, and how and when you will evaluate the progress. (As an added component, since this involves men holding the office of deacon, you may discuss the extra challenge this conflict includes since those who should be aiding in church unity may be contributing to its disunity.) You may supplement your answer with other information and sources, but be sure to include information from our study in chapter 13, especially as it relates to biblical example and mandate for conflict resolution.

Chapter 14

Exploring Risk in the Local Church

Developing a comprehensive risk management plan for both the church and its ministries is an essential component of wise leadership. Liabilities surrounding mandatory reporting, allegations of abuse, facilities, trips, emergencies, and the threat of active shooters are now a common part of ministry conversations. Any given week, I am questioned about the potential for an active shooting incident during a worship service, broken homes and the ensuing custody battles of children attending church, or the risk factors of an upcoming event. Similarly, in a changing culture, gender identity, suicide, bullying, mental health, and potential harm are concerns as people go to work and school, and these issues also affect the church. In this chapter, we cannot address all the circumstances or provide a step-by-step plan to handle all the risks we could encounter in ministry. However, we can provide some thoughts about assessment and planning to provide a foundation for your local church to develop a comprehensive plan. A well-thought-out risk-management plan allows leaders to respond wisely rather than react foolishly to incidences as they occur.

The principle that guides my personal philosophy for risk management is that of a shepherd who protects their flock, whether from within the fold or from an outside threat. When I was in college, I worked at a department store for a season and was shocked to learn that 42 percent of theft was employee-related. Some employees would simply wear new clothes and shoes home. Loss prevention was tasked with securing the store from inside and outside threats. The church should have the same mindset of looking both within and without, considering all the risk factors for protecting the church as a structure, organization, and community of believers.

Anytime we gather for worship, Bible study, or a special event, there is some level of inherent risk. Five to ten years ago, ministry leaders did not consider today's most pressing issues as notable or concerning. Risk management is a changing aspect of church leadership that requires ongoing assessment and learning. As ministry leaders, helping your people understand and navigate these issues can be challenging. Smaller, family-oriented churches are particularly averse to addressing potential risk, since they are closely related or tend to know one another very well. Even a small church can be surprised with an incident from an unsuspecting church member or person in the community. The phrase "a wolf in sheep's clothing" can also apply to this topic with mandatory reporting, background checks, recruiting volunteers and chaperones, and how church discipline is navigated. Each of the issues needs to be considered. You should be having conversations in your church among ministry leaders on how to address and process the risk factors, whether concerning finances, people, or facilities. You may not need a policy or procedure for each aspect, but you do need a critical leadership team that continues to pray over, consider, and recommend a risk-management plan for your church.

You may be thinking, *where should I begin to tackle the umbrella of risk for a church?* The first step is to divide the work into categories: people, insurance, activities and events, and property. From there we will take a closer look at the challenges, opportunities, and essential elements of risk management within each category.

People

The challenge with navigating risks when we lead ministries is centered around people. Facilities, outside threats, and finances carry risks, but the main dangers we face are people both within and outside the church. When you consider the following aspects of protecting the church, remember the crucial resource for any church is the people. If you have volunteers who cannot arrive early or lack a desire to be involved in training, then a risk strategy will be an ongoing challenge that could even contribute to more significant risks. If a risk team for security is only half staffed on a Sunday morning, then half of your plan is not staffed or ready to protect the people. You have created a false sense of preparedness, and as a result, the people are more exposed by assuming the church is better prepared for potential threats than they are ready to combat. In a connected society with social media and church websites, we have given the world access to our local congregations. I enjoyed three church services through livestreams recently when I was at home sick. The convenience of being connected at a distance is a great benefit to us in our everyday life. Still, it has also allowed people who could cause harm to know our schedule, events, things to consider as first-time guests, floorplan or map of facilities, and even names and faces of the people. Digital information can cause the church to be vulnerable to a threat from someone outside of the church.

Insurance

When I think of insurance, the types of coverages are one component to ensure you are insured for the overall risks associated with what you do each week. The people component deals with volunteers, staff, contractors, ministry organization partners, and attendees, both members and guests. Property is what you own, rent, borrow, or utilize to do your ministry's work. People rent cabins, contract retreat centers for a special event, lease a banquet space, rent transportation, lease equipment, and buy equipment that can be categorized as property. The property can be extended beyond the buildings and land the church owns or rents. In most people's minds, they think of property solely as the church's facility for worship, Bible study, and weekly ministry. Property, as a whole, encompasses every type of physical, church-owned land or building and has to be considered for risk.

Activities and Events

Activities and events can be confusing for the church because you have ongoing weekly activities and special events. We'll use the term *activity* to describe weekly programs like an ongoing Wednesday night children's group or weekly praise band rehearsal. An event would be more occasional, like a discipleship weekend, vacation Bible school, or a revival—a targeted time that occurs more annually than weekly. Some events can be covered by special event insurance and do not require ongoing coverage. Many churches now have social media accounts, websites, online giving, and apps for the church and its ministries. These aspects add a new area of insurance coverage that should be considered. It is also vital to consider the element of covering the church's volunteers and staff when they are employed to fulfill a specific ministry assignment. Many aspects exist to an insurance policy, and while some have been highlighted here for you, every church should always review their total coverage throughout the year. The insurance agent can walk you through each aspect of your coverage and explain them; however, each insurance element comes with a cost. The amount of coverage, areas of coverage, and the total umbrella coverage amount have to review what a church can afford and cannot afford not to be covered for in the church's work. This reveals the picture of insuring a church for the place and ministries that occur routinely and special events within the property and buildings the church uses weekly for the church to exist.

Property

Protecting the church property can be confusing as the lines can get blurred quickly. A church youth group contracts a retreat center for a weekend. The church opens the event to other churches but is beyond the scope of why the church exists and places the church as an owner renting or lending their property to others. When one allows others to use their facility, the insurance may not extend to the other groups or the facilities' use.

Safety during events and throughout your space is a challenge when there are different smaller groups, such as women's Bible study or college worship time, happening at times when the building is not normally open. As you schedule the calendar, always take a few extra steps by thinking about safety for the event. As we move to highlight some specific topics related to risk, a few terms will be essential for you. You'll need to consider the terms *avoid, defer, share,* and *transfer* anytime you plan to do anything as a church. You can avoid the risk by eliminating events or areas of concern that you deem too risky without limiting your church's ministry. You could defer the risk by delaying an event or ministry until you are more prepared with equipped leaders and volunteers to navigate the risk. Sometimes it is appropriate to share the risk by partnering with another organization for an event. You may use a para-church ministry for a camp instead of planning your own, and thus you share the risk. You could transfer the risk altogether for transportation and charter your travel with a licensed and insured company. We cannot eliminate the factors of risk in what we do, but we can reduce or manage this area to church life. We will always have activity, people, medical, and facility risk as we minister to people and plan the church's work to corporate worship, reach, and disciple people each week.

Risk Assessment

You may be asking, "So where do I begin to assess potential risks within the church beyond the scope of our insurance coverage?" I recommend evaluating the weekly schedule, calendared ministry components, and the outside organizations that will utilize your facilities. Then conduct an assessment of your church's scheduled ministries, activities, and events. Several insurance companies for churches have resources to help you review your actions, facilities, and programs. I utilize tools and resources from Guidestone, Brotherhood Mutual, and Church Mutual to help me regularly review forms, checklists, safety, and security processes and a trusted source with Church Tax and Law Update as the culture changes around us. This is not a formal endorsement of these companies, but they each have resources to help you further review, tweak, and protect your church and the ministries offered. While risk cannot be eliminated, it can be shared, transferred, or reduced. The cultural environment that we live with has catchy commercials and billboards for lawyers seeking to help people who have been injured or endangered by someone or their property. This means our people, property, and activities need us to be a shepherd who casts a watchful eye on protecting our people and the church's ministries.

Risk Assessment: Property

Scenario: High Ropes Accident

At a leased retreat center, the invited speaker participates in high ropes recreation when an accident occurs, and several are injured. The retreat nor the church completed an accident report. All are treated with minor first aid at the event. The next week a lawyer contacts the church seeking details on a victim's family. Their son will need ongoing physical therapy and possible surgery from injuries sustained during the retreat that were not reported to the family during the weekend event. The youth minister signed the contract and secured the speaker without trustees in the church reviewing the contracts. The church insurance now will have to decide if they will work with the church since the agreement was not executed according to the church bylaws for trustees to manage contracts and cover the youth minister named in the process.

While I am not a lawyer or insurance adjuster, the youth ministry event could be replaced with an incident at vacation Bible school, a fall festival, or during a weekly time of ministry at your church around a worship service.

Risk Assessment: People

Scenario: The Intriguing Visitor

A man arrives dressed in black with a backpack. He fits the profile of someone who desires to disrupt or cause harm. He passes by the first-impression team in the parking lot and arrives in the foyer to meet a cautious greeter. The security team is alerted, and the man is confronted in the worship space. He is asked to come to the foyer, where three men explain the concerns and ask to inspect his bag. It turns out he is a first-time guest, who is indeed homeless, carrying all his possessions in an overstuffed backpack. As a ministry leader, you begin to wonder if this was a case of unfair profiling when the church family should have been more welcoming. Do the people's actions reveal that this could have been a person on another Sunday who would desire to cause harm?

The challenges any given week are real, and you have to be trained to be carefully ministerial without being a profiler who prevents people from coming. While I don't have a perfect explanation for how to interact with intriguing visitors, I do know we must pray for wisdom and help others exercise discernment. A line from a hymn should remind us as Christians, we are "safe and secure from all alarms." I grew up singing "Leaning on the Everlasting Arms." As we approach a ministry of security, we need to lean on his arms and not our own. However, as leaders, we have to be vigilant in knowing the real threats within our congregation and those outside the church's walls.

Risk Assessment: Property

Scenario: Check-In Challenge
The youth meet in the older part of the building away from the main gathering points in the church. The youth space is furnished with donated family room furniture and a few gently used pool tables,

rickety Ping-Pong tables, and some other games to try and engage the next generation. Each week the youth begin arriving an hour before the Wednesday worship time begins. After service, a mother appears, wondering why her daughter did not come to the car after youth group. The youth minister does not recall the girl attending, but the mother states that the family had a Wednesday night meal together in the fellowship hall. People begin trying to call, text, and search for this fifteen-year-old girl. She may have left with friends between the meal and youth group. She could have been abducted between buildings since you walk through an exterior courtyard from the fellowship hall and the youth room. No one knows where she is, but she was last seen on the church property at some point earlier in the evening.

You may have experienced a similar circumstance. The church in this scenario does not keep up with attendance beyond preschool, offering a straightforward check-in and check-out for minors. We all dream what it would be to design and build facilities with a blank slate in light of the new realities of doing ministry week in and week out. Most of us, however, are tasked with creating a safe environment in our current church building. We simply cannot overlook systems for the safety and care of minors. Although we can dream about what we would like, the reality is we have to live with what we have. Be creative and find ways to mitigate the risk involving everyone under the age of eighteen.

Risk Assessment: Activities

Scenario: The Touch of a Stranger
Picture this: a church setting that is striving to do ministry well and is always short on volunteers.

Generally, whoever is available covers the need and keeps the ministries going each week. The reality of canceling a ministry due to a lack of volunteers is not a call a minister wants to make. The children's ministry is always understaffed but gets by to survive another Sunday until an unfortunate incident occurs. A child attending Sunday school tells her mom on the way home from church that a stranger touched her in a way that made her feel uncomfortable. After asking a few questions, the mother realizes this is an older member who has faithfully served the church most of his life. Regardless, the mother calls the pastor that afternoon and asks to meet with him about her concerns.

Many adults like to explain these encounters away and not follow the mandatory reporting guidelines of their state. Families will even rationalize that the girl simply was mistaken. However, the minister is responsible not to be a mandatory *investigator* to the allegation but a mandatory *reporter*. Regardless of church size or location, a wise leader will know, understand, and follow the mandatory reporting guidelines to which they are accountable.

Mandatory reporting is a legal process for reporting any abuse that is shared with a ministry leader. One website that can help you understand this more is www.childwelfare .gov/topics/systemwide/laws-policies/statutes/manda/. Brotherhood Mutual also offers this advice: "The term 'mandatory reporter' refers to those who are required by state law to report suspected abuse or other dangerous behavior. These individuals generally face criminal penalties if they fail to report such activity. You need to consult the local laws in your area for what aspects fall into the mandatory reporting designation. . . . For example, in some states, everyone is considered a mandatory child abuse reporter."[127]

Additional Considerations

What about our digital platforms?

In a world where people stay connected through many streams and services, online connectivity is an aspect each church must consider for safety, security, liability, and accountability. Consider your online platform a digital ministry space and facility for risk management. Digital ministry often occurs via platforms such as Facebook, YouTube, church apps and websites, or a variety of others sources.[128] However, you should consider these components for ministry strategy and effectiveness as well. Whether an app, social media page, website, online giving platform, or digital event, the church-sponsored media carries unique challenges and risks that merit a use plan, accountability for unwanted interaction, hacking, and protection for minors as well as adults.

Streaming worship services is standard for many churches today, but the interaction around those services needs accountability. The ministries that share about minors and interact with children need to have similar controls and protections as those we have when gathered in physical space.

---

[127] "What Should Ministry Personnel Know About Mandatory Reporting Requirements?" Brotherhood Mutual, https://www.brotherhoodmutual .com/legalassist/legal-q-a/ministry-activities-and-operations/q -what-should-ministry-personnel-know-about-mandatory-reporting -requirements/.

[128] Consider this website for more information: Ryan Wakefield, "The Ultimate List of Social Media Policies for Churches & Ministries," Church Marketing University, https://socialchurch.co/social-media-policies -churches-ministries/.

Does insurance cover our staff, volunteers, and facilities?

Insurance for staff, volunteers, and facilities can be a challenge. When a church does not have someone who routinely reviews the church policies for facility coverage and types of coverage, it can find it is lacking coverage in an area that could have existed previously or changed in the policy renewal. A policy can be altered before renewal due to changes in the region due to weather events or other cultural challenges. The policy should cover property replacement at the level of facility you have and not a base per square foot essential replacement cost.

You'll need an inventory of your contents, including media equipment, office equipment, library content, staff belongings, and expensive furnishings from a chandelier in the foyer to the grand piano. The list seems endless on types of coverage and areas of consideration. Consider what coverage your church needs to protect and care for facilities, volunteers, and paid staff, including how internet exposure could also cause need for liability coverage, as well as church borrowed, rented, or owned transportation. More extensive one week or one-day events can be covered with special event insurance if you add the coverage before the event occurs. You should develop a strong relationship with your insurance agent and ask questions about your policy.

What are important considerations during our weekly gatherings?

Security for anyone and at any time you gather should always be considered because people walk around even when no one is there. Regardless of whether you are in an urban or rural environment, the reality is someone can cause harm at any time. These security issues could include someone breaking into cars during church meetings and worship or a homeless person looking for a warm place to sleep. Simply take a few moments each week to review the calendar and consider the security for each. You can make a checklist to help in the assessment, including everything from outdoor lighting to locking the facility.

Should church finances be considered when completing risk assessment?

Finances are an area that people may not associate with risk, but many aspects in this area can be problematic. Fiscal responsibility with who has access to funds, records, and reports can be an issue. You should have a process for accounting and auditing the church records for finance—a method for how funds can be spent and who has the authority to approve those expenditures. You do not need everyone to have access to records. Still, a few people with integrity and accountability need to have the ability to review the current state of finances and the last three or so years and provide a forecast for cash flow and expenses.

How do I assess risk related to severe weather or health emergencies?

Emergencies can relate to weather, health, people, or the facility. Any given week, a severe weather threat could happen in your region. People have health concerns such as heart attacks, stroke, or incidental injuries that may evolve into a personal health emergency. We have become more aware of community-wide health concerns that could potentially harm the group at large. People can cause harm or have family emergencies that impact the church's ministry, and we have to be sensitive to these needs. A facility can have troubles any given day from an overflowing toilet to structural damage that needs immediate attention. These emergencies require a response, but each needs a clear, thought-out plan with people trained to respond to the specific area of emergency.

How do I ensure our church transportation is safe and secure?

Transportation can be where you transfer the risk to another by chartering a driver and vehicle to transport your people for ministry events and trips. You may share the risk by renting the transportation but providing vetted drivers for the ministry event or trip. Many churches decide to own, rent, and charter based on the size of the event. Be sure to vet the company for their safety record and insurance. If you rent, conduct pre-trip inspections and follow advised safety protocols. When you own a vehicle, complete an application and approval protocol for drivers. Be sure to have a maintenance plan and protocols for usage of the church-owned vehicles. Always follow your plan and document the evidence of maintenance, driver vetting, and pre-trip inspections. Always follow current guidelines to operate transportation as safely as possible.

Is it safe to allow outside groups to use our facilities for events or gatherings?

Many churches have facilities that are not used every day of the week, and outside organizations may ask to borrow, rent, or partner with the church to use the worship center, gym, or other church areas. Always ask why and what the content of their program will be to align with the church. If you simply loan the facility, then still complete a facility use form and ask for an insurance certificate that lists the church by name on their policy. When you rent, also follow church guidelines, but remember the church becomes the place that is the provider of a service, which includes liability. Policies and procedures should be outlined for how and what the facilities can be utilized. Outline the costs for renting, cleaning, and even repair costs for damages. If you outline a process and ministry guidelines informed by scripture, then even weddings and funerals will be covered under this process and outside organizations.

How do I mitigate risk with online giving? Isn't it just safer to pass the plate?

As the world continues to move more online through their business operations with online giving, protecting people's personal information, securing Wi-Fi, and teaching people how to be good stewards of technology has many challenges. You can carry insurance coverage for your online business for website, giving, and online business records. I would encourage you to teach your people how to manage their media use and protect their families from the threat presented with online gaming, social media, and apps. Pushpay through Church Community Builder is a great resource for online giving.[129]

How do we complete background checks for volunteers? Does everyone need a background check? It's so expensive.

Each church has to decide who can serve with minors and in what capacities. Many churches make the decision that only

---

[129] Church analytics may be an area you would like to explore further. See www.churchlytics.com. It offers advice on church software and online giving that may be helpful to you and your ministry.

church members can lead a Bible study group. A church may not be as rigid for recreation when they need a coach for a kid's team, a chaperone for camp, or volunteers for vacation Bible school. A straightforward process for volunteers to have a criminal background check, and even a social media background check, would be wise. This process would begin with a volunteer application for anyone who desires to serve. I have used Ministry Safe and Protect My Ministry, and these two have proven time and again to be valuable options for aiding in ministries with minors.

The world continues to change, and as ministry leaders, we must be people who do our due diligence to protect the church and its people from harm at all stages of life. The challenges and aspects cannot be addressed in a few thousand words but have been offered as a way for you to broaden your thinking and research and look for ways to improve in the risk-management aspects associated with ministry. If you need to ask a follow-up question, please visit my website jodyddean.wordpress.com.

About the Authors

Adam Hughes, having seventeen years of experience in the local church, teaches courses in preaching, leadership, and pastoral ministries at New Orleans Baptist Theological Seminary (NOBTS). His writing has appeared on the websites for Preaching Source and Theology Matters. He also has been a contributor to several works including *Small Church, Excellent Ministry: A Guidebook for Pastors* and *Together We Equip*. Most recently he wrote "The Soul of the Evangelistic Expository Sermon: From Broadus and Criswell to Rogers and Kelley" in the 2019 publication *Engage: Tools for Contemporary Evangelism*. He is also cohost of *Pastor to Pastor*, a weekly podcast through the ministry of NOBTS. He and his wife, Holly, have four children.

Jody Dean, having more than twenty years of experience in the local church, teaches courses in administration, risk management, and discipleship at New Orleans Baptist Theological Seminary. As editor of *Together We Equip* and author of *Protect*, as well as a contributor to several other works, he has a desire to help ministry leaders and lay leaders be equipped for serving the church. He and his wife, Emily, have two children.

IRON
STREAM
MEDIA

If you enjoyed this book, will you consider sharing the message with others?

Let us know your thoughts. You can let the author know by visiting or sharing a photo of the cover on our social media pages or leaving a review at a retailer's site. All of it helps us get the message out!

Email: info@ironstreammedia.com

 @ironstreammedia

Brookstone Publishing Group, Harambee Press, Iron Stream, Iron Stream Fiction, Iron Stream Kids, and Life Bible Study are imprints of Iron Stream Media, which derives its name from Proverbs 27:17, "As iron sharpens iron, so one person sharpens another." This sharpening describes the process of discipleship, one to another. With this in mind, Iron Stream Media provides a variety of solutions for churches, ministry leaders, and nonprofits ranging from in-depth Bible study curriculum and Christian book publishing to custom publishing and consultative services.

For more information on ISM and its imprints, please visit IronStreamMedia.com